KU-316-685

Teaching all the children to read

Concentrated language encounter techniques

RICHARD WALKER,
SAOWALAK RATTANAVICH AND
JOHN W. OLLER, Jr

Open University Press
Buckingham · Philadelphia

Open University Press
Celtic Court
22 Ballmoor
Buckingham
MK18 1XW

and
1900 Frost Road, Suite 101
Bristol, PA 19007, USA

First Published 1992

LEEDS METROPOLITAN
UNIVERSITY LIBRARY

1701488263

B13C

457489

428.61 WAL

19 AUG 1996   £10.99 INV

Copyright © Richard Walker, Saowalak Rattanavich and John W. Oller, Jr 1992

All rights reserved. No part of this publication may be
reproduced, stored in a retrieval system or transmitted in
any form or by any means, without written permission from the
publisher.

A catalogue record of this book is available
from the British Library

Library of Congress Cataloging-in-Publication Data

Walker, Richard, 1925–
    Teaching all the children to read : concentrated language
encounter techniques / Richard Walker, Saowalak Rattanavich & John
Oller.
     p.   cm. — (Rethinking reading)
    Includes index.
    ISBN 0–335–15729–7   ISBN 0–335–15728–9 (pbk.)
    1. Reading (Elementary)—Developing countries.   2. Literacy—
Developing countries.   3. Classroom management—Developing
countries.   I. Rattanavich, Saowalak, 1951–   .   II. Oller, John W.
III. Title.   IV. Series.
LB1573.W313   1992
372.4'1—dc20   92–8566
                                                   CIP

Typeset by Inforum, Rowlands Castle, Hants
Printed in Great Britain by St Edmundsbury Press,
Bury St Edmunds, Suffolk

Contents

Acknowledgements

The authors of this book find themselves with two roles. The first is as spokespersons for those who developed what has come to be known as the approach to teaching language and literacy. The second is as recorders for the large and varied group of people in Thailand who, recognizing its potential, embraced the large-scale application of that approach in a nationwide programme.

Foremost among the former is Brian Gray, now senior lecturer in education at the University of Canberra, Australia. Brian was director of the curriculum project, at Traeger Park School, in which the concentrated language encounter (CLE) methodology was developed. He has maintained contact with the work in Thailand by contributing to the training of key personnel; and the Thai project team regard him as a good friend. We know, also, that Brian and those who worked with him at the Traeger Park School would want us to pay tribute to the late Graeme Cooper, former principal of that school. Graeme was the rock on which the Traeger Park CLE project was founded. He was closely involved with Thai key personnel whom he extended hospitality to in Darwin just a few weeks before his untimely death in late 1990.

Others who contributed to the training of key personnel for the Thai CLE work, both in Thailand and Australia, and thereby influenced the directions in which that work developed, were Professor Frances Christie of the University of the Northern Territory, and Dr Nea Stewart-Dore and Dr Brendan Bartlett, of the Brisbane College of Advanced Education (now Griffith University), Australia. The role played by Dr John Chapman, of the Open University, UK, is noted within the pages of this book.

Above all, we should like to acknowledge the work of those from the Srinakharinwirot University, from the Thai Ministry of Education, and the Rotarians of Thailand who took the CLE methodology and from it built a complete programme for primary schools, developed a teacher-training system, and set up the basis from which to disseminate CLE language teaching techniques, nationwide and abroad. No acknowledgement that we could make would adequately reflect our admiration for the vision, the courage and the energy of Dr Chatri Muangnapoe, Rector of the Srinakharinwirot University, Dr Aree Sanhahawee, past principal of the Demonstration School at Prasarnmit Campus of Srinakharinwirot University, or of Associate Professors Hearthai Tandjong and Chari Suvathi who played continuing direct roles in book development, teacher training and assessment.

Much of what is recounted in this book could never have occurred without the cooperation and encouragement of Dr Komel Phuprasert, of the Office of National Primary Education, Ministry of Education in Thailand, and of Mr Phanom Keokamnerd, a former senior officer of that ministry.

Special acknowledgement is due to Rotary District Governor Nominee Mr Noraseth Pathmanand, the Rotary Chairman of the project over its full five years, to Past Rotary Governor Krisda Arunvongse Na Ayuthaya, who began the work and who, with Rotary Director Bhichai Rattakul and Past Governors Praphan Hutasingh and Mom Rachawongsee Ophas Kanchanavijaya, has maintained a special interest throughout.

It is with warmth and affection that we acknowledge the efforts of close friends and colleagues in Thailand who could truly be said to have written this book, because they did what is recorded within it. Among them are Rotarians Thawatchai Sutibongkot, Preecha Klinkaeo, Chaiyasit Kositapai, Rudi Areesorn, Vinai Sachdev and Howard Mirkin. Others who made outstanding contributions to this work include members of the Ministry of Education team, Praphapan Nil-aroon, Surat Jatakul, Aksorn Praserd, Sa-Ard Sasitharamas and Sanan Meekharnmark.

We would especially like to thank Susan Pike, of SCECGS School, Sydney, for her contribution to the CLE English-language project and for her hospitality to the Thai author in Australia during the writing of this book. Finally, we should like to acknowledge the long and enduring involvement of Fay Walker. Whether it was in Thailand or Australia, in visiting schools or in caring for visitors from Thailand, she was always there to help and support.

CHAPTER 1

General introduction

RICHARD WALKER

Introduction

The general expectation is that people who have had six or more years of formal education can read and write; but that is far from the case. Even in countries that have had universal education for generations there are substantial numbers of illiterates[1], and everywhere a worrying number of children leave school each year with reading difficulties that will adversely affect their future. Actual failure rates vary, of course, but figures above 50 per cent are not uncommon in some places.

What people need to be able to read and write, if they are to lead satisfying and satisfactory lives, also varies from place to place. But it is not unrealistic to expect that the great majority of students will finish their school years with the literacy skills they need as they enter adult life. That is surely no more unreasonable than to expect children to learn to speak their language well enough to cope with everyday demands, before they begin school at the age of five or six years. Indeed, one would be hard-put to make the case that the latter is the easier task. However, the failure rate in learning to speak a language at home, is much lower than in learning to read and write at school.

This book is about developing school programmes that will enable virtually all children to learn to read and write. We believe that all schools, everywhere, can and should do that for all its students, whatever their language background or their prior experience with literacy activities.

This first chapter begins with a review of some of the reasons put forward to account for high literacy failure rates in schools. Then it presents glimpses of Mary, a child who would normally fail to learn to read, and whose failure would be attributed to mistaken reasons. Finally, it introduces *concentrated language encounter* (CLE) – literacy teaching techniques that have enabled Mary and a wide range of other children, who faced almost inevitable failure, to succeed in school.

Reasons why many children fail to learn to read

Children from actively literate families have developed all or most of the essential understandings about reading and writing from literacy experiences during their early childhood – many of them to the extent that they have already begun to read before they come to school (Smith and Johnson, 1976: 28). On the other hand, those who begin school with little or no prior experience of written language are faced with an unfamiliar language code. They still have in front of them the full task of puzzling out its nature, its various forms and conventions, and its uses and usefulness. Researchers such as Wells (1981) have shown that these latter children are the more likely to fail to learn to read and write.

High failure rates in learning to read are also found among minority populations, in which case linguistic and other cultural factors are given as causes of failure, as well as literacy background. Children for whom the language of instruction is a second language or second dialect are seen as having the doubly difficulty task of learning to participate in the spoken as well as the written discourse of the classroom.

As is discussed in Chapter 6, multiple difficulties of that kind exist among rural and city slum populations in many developing countries.

It has even been suggested that failure to learn to read and write is merely inabilty 'to meet their parents' or teachers' expectations in reading' (Smith and Johnson, 1976: 33). The view is that a substantial proportion of school reading failures should be accepted because there will always be students who perform at worse than average level. Reading is seen as 'an intellectual activity' that less able children will not be able to cope with until they reach some predetermined stage of intellectual growth. Teachers are urged to use programmes that 'postpone actual reading activities and move children more slowly through the developmental reading process' (Smith and Johnson, 1976: 38). We are reminded of parents who won't let their children enter the water until they can swim.

Whether it be 15 per cent of the population of an industrialized country, a larger proportion of a minority group, or an even larger proportion of the children who live in a remote region of a developing country, it is unacceptable to use family or language background to explain away a high failure rate. Rather, the known likelihood of failure should enliven a search for ways of preventing it.

The authors believe that the basic reasons why so many school children fail to learn to read have more to do with what goes on in schools than

with what the children bring to school. Certainly, there are pupil characteristics that correlate with failure in the kinds of literacy teaching that
currently go on in schools but that ceases to exist when appropriate
changes are made to the school context for learning and teaching. School
learning environments can be created that suit the full range of students,
and not just those whose family backgrounds fit them for what currently
goes on in schools.

The CLE techniques that are described in this book do indeed suit a
much wider range of children than do conventional programmes, and the
authors believe that they offer much to the theory and practice of literacy
teaching.

'Mary', a child who is destined to fail

The fundamental principles of CLE language/literacy teaching were
worked out in a search for solutions to gross failure among Aboriginal
students at Traeger Park School, in the Northern Territory of Australia
(Gray, 1983).

Mary was a beginning student at that school and the following transcripts reveal the contrast between her language behaviour in the kind of
teacher–child language interaction that normally goes on in schools and in
other kinds of contexts, including the kind of classroom interaction that
marks CLE teaching. The transcripts are from recordings of Mary and her
classmates that were made in a language research project, soon after they
began school (Walker, 1981).

Mary is an accomplished linguist in that she speaks a dialect of English
as well as an Aboriginal first language. In English, she can understand what
is said to her and make herself understood but she will almost inevitably fail
in school and her teachers will attribute her failure mainly to inability to
communicate with her in English.

Transcript A is of an interaction between Mary and her classroom
teacher. Mary and her friend Jane are sitting side by side on the classroom
floor, where they have been making things out of coloured rods and 'fit on'
wooden shapes, in a free activity period at the beginning of a school day.

Transcript A

Teacher: What are you making Mary? (No response)
What are you making? (No response)
Very nice (examining Mary's construction).
What's this part? Is that pink? (Mary shakes her head)
No? What is it? (No response) Blue?
Mary: Yeah.

Teacher:	Mm. It's blue. What's this one here?
Mary:	Blue.
Teacher:	Good. That's blue. What's this one? Yellow? (Mary nods her head) Can you see another yellow one? (Mary points) Very good. (This procedure is repeated for other colours) What are you doing now, Mary? (No response) What are you doing love? (No response) Are you putting it together? Building something? (No response. Mary goes on working)
Mary:	(As she works) Making chair.
Teacher:	Making a chair? Oh? Who's the chair for?
Mary:	Sitting down.
Teacher:	For sitting down? Oh. Who's going to sit on it? (No response) Is Jane going to sit on the chair or you? (No response) Who's going to sit on it?
Mary:	Jane.

In that conversation, a teacher is working hard to establish communication with Mary. She tries to teach the names for objects and colours, on the basis of Mary's own activity, or to test whether Mary already has those concepts and the English labels for them.

The teacher's first try at a language exchange requires Mary only to name the object she has been making but Mary does not respond even to a second trial of that probe. The teacher tries to establish a better interpersonal relationship by praising the chair that Mary has built. She then tries to make her next question a more specific one – the colour of a part of the chair. The demand on Mary is made as light as possible by naming the colour and asking only for affirmation or negation. Mary replies with a shake of her head and on that basis, the teacher tries, more ambitiously, to get Mary to supply the name of the colour. That fails, and the teacher goes back to requiring only affirmation or negation.

She now makes some progress because Mary uses her voice for the first time, to say 'Yeah' and even says the word 'blue' after the teacher has used it. The teacher then goes back to requiring affirmation only and pointing out other pieces of the same colour.

Apparently encouraged by this cooperative turn-taking by Mary, the teacher then goes back to her original gambit of asking what Mary is doing but that fails entirely, even when the question is reframed to require only affirmation or negation.

The teacher seems to think that Mary's problem may lie in inability to understand the verb she is using. Notice that she uses 'making', 'doing', 'putting together', and 'building' for the one process, in her various attempts to elicit a response. Mary understood her first try, as far as terminology was concerned, because a little later, she volunteered 'making chair'.

The picture is of a teacher fighting hard for a basis for language communication with Mary, but being forced to a lower and lower level of demand. The communication she actually achieved resembles that with a child who has virtually no English. Mary seems either unable or unwilling to communicate on a level of complexity above that of the simplest of concepts and language labels.

But Transcript B, which is a record of playground interaction on the same day, reveals that Mary can operate at a level of English language usage far above what she has revealed to the teacher. Mary is sharing a double push-pull swing with Sue. The two girls are sitting on the same seat, one behind the other, with Mary in front and in control of the push-pull bars. Two other girls are sharing a similar swing nearby, and a fifth is dancing around the swings, awaiting a turn.

Transcript B

Mary: On again. On here again. Me push.

(To Sue) Look, you push me. You push.

(To the other pair of girls) We'll go really fast like you.

(To Sue) Like this, eh?

Hey, Marilyn fall down and . . . (Telling the fifth girl to repeat the trick she's just done).

Move back Sue (Mary is slipping off the front of the seat). No. You, no. Hey Sue (annoyed because Sue slipped along the seat). I'll take you really fast. Sue, you thing (annoyed that Sue is wriggling around).

(Both get off the swing). Me turn. Jane and me and Jane now. Me and Jane now. You and me.

(To the other girls) You and Sue at the back. Jane, other side, other side.

In this playground episode, Mary is garrulous and dominant to the extent that no one else has a turn to speak. More significantly, her dominance of the others is achieved and maintained through using English. Clearly, she can use English confidently and powerfully in this kind of context.

At the end of the day, in free classroom time before leaving for home, Mary is playing with large coloured beads on the floor, and we get some additional insights into Mary's ability to interact in English.

Transcript C

Mary: The colours, the colours, colours. (Bill, a classmate, moves over to her and annoys her) I'll tell on you.

Vera: Bill Brown, leave her alone.

Mary: (To Bill) I'll tell on you. (Calling softly, as a threat to Bill) Mrs
Peters! I'll tell on you, Bill. You're making troubles. You're making
troubles, not me. (Continues playing) All the colours, all the
colours.

From Transcript C, we learn that Mary is sufficiently aware of the
dynamics of classroom control to use the teacher's authority as a threat and
to attribute blame for a breach of behavioural requirements. Finally, we are
struck with Mary's almost poetic use of language to express her feelings
about the colours of the beads and it becomes evident, too, that her use of
English is spontaneous and effortless, as she works away alone in the
classroom.

Other occasions were recorded of Mary's teachers making very earnest
attempts to draw Mary into normal teacher–pupil instructional dialogue
but every time, by perfectly logical steps, they fell into dialogue of the
adult–infant type, in which the adult provides the answer that is required
from the child. The teachers received no indication that Mary would ever
participate in classroom discourse in which meaning is negotiated through
language.

In all the transcripts, Mary's teachers seem to be unaware that Mary
can use English at a higher level of functioning. They act always as if Mary is
almost without language. On her part, Mary is unwilling to take risks. She
won't respond to questions put to her by a teacher unless the answer has
already been supplied.

It seems obvious that these teachers will eventually accept Mary's non-
participation, except for sporadic efforts to communicate with her at a level
of sophistication well below that used with non-Aboriginal children. Mary is
well on the way to a permanent role of a non-participant in most of what
goes on in the classroom. She can take a very active role in the games that
are played outside but she cannot play the one that is being played in the
classroom.

But what happens if that classroom game is changed? Transcript D was
recorded on the next morning but it is from a 'concentrated language
encounter' session – one of the first that was devised at Traeger Park
School to bring Aboriginal children into classroom learning. For about the
third time, the children are making toast together in a corner of the school
language unit.

Transcript D

Bill: Can I put some butter?

Teacher: We have to wait first until the toaster is ready to pop up. What
colour do you think the bread will be when it pops up? What
colour?

Bill:	Brown.
Mary:	Brown.
Teacher:	Brown. That's right.
Mary:	It pop up.
Sally:	I can smell it now.
Teacher:	(To the other children) Can you smell it?
Mary:	(Enjoying the smell of toast) Hey!
Teacher:	Does it make you feel hungry, Mary?
Mary:	(Nods her head) My mother got peanut butter.
Teacher:	Your mother's got peanut butter, has she?
Bill:	We got some peanut butter home.
Teacher:	You've got peanut butter at home too?
Bill:	Yeah, and one of these.
Teacher:	And a toaster.
Mary:	And one of these.
Teacher:	(To Mary) What's that called? (Interrupted by the toaster popping) Oh it's popped up.
Mary:	Black now. It's black.
Teacher:	D'you think it's burnt?
Mary:	Yeah.
Teacher:	I think it's probably all right.
Mary:	(Excited) It's black. Black. It's black.
Teacher:	Dinner time. Yes. It's dinner time.
Mary:	Dinner time. Dinner time.
Teacher:	Take the toast out of the toaster now, Bill. (Bill does so) What are we going to do now, Mary?
Mary:	Clean it.
Teacher:	(Surprised) We're going to clean it?
Mary:	(Demonstrating) This way.
Sally:	Scrape it. Scrape it.
Teacher:	Why do we have to scrape it?
Mary:	It's yucky!
Sally:	With the knife.
Teacher:	No, that's all right! (Thinks the toast doesn't need scraping) Then what do you have to do? What are we going to put on it now?
Mary:	Peanut butter.
Teacher:	What are we going to put on it before we put peanut butter?
Mary:	Butter.
Teacher:	Good girl! Come on, then, you spread this – a nice piece of toast. Bill's going to put some butter on the other slice of toast.
Mary:	This one?

Teacher:	Yes, good girl! Do you help your mother to butter the toast at home, Mary?
Mary:	(Nods)
Teacher:	What's happening to the butter?
Lynette:	It'll melt.
Teacher:	It's melting. That's right, because the toast is hot. This (the butter container) feels nice and cold.
Lynette:	I take it. I take it. (Picks up the butter container to feel it)
Teacher:	The toast melts the butter.
Mary:	It's melting. Look there. It's melting. Look.
Lynette:	Mine melting too. (Looking at Mary's toast)

Note how markedly different Mary's language participation is here from what it was in Transcript A, although the same teacher and the same children are involved, and the transcripts were recorded on consecutive days. Not only does Mary now respond confidently to teacher questions, she also initiates interaction. Even more usefully, she is prepared to adopt and argue a point of view about whether or not the toast should be 'scraped'. There is a much more substantive communicative basis for teaching Mary than in Transcript A.

To those who worked with Mary, the reasons for the change gradually became clear. Because she has shared in toast-making on previous mornings, she is familiar with it: the names of things, what is done with them, and the sequence in which things are done.

She also knows what will be demanded of her in the role of toast-maker, because she's seen others take turns as central participants. Finally, she has realized that all the language demands made on her in this session will be based on her role in the toast-making.

In other words, Mary can interpret all that is said and done within the context of toast-making, herself as toast-maker, and the teacher as organizer/supervisor of that activity. And she has no trouble relating language elements and structures to reality, because the toast-making process and the related language have both been repeatedly modelled, one along with the other.

It is interesting to note, too, that Mary makes a dialectal switch during this session. When she volunteers her first pieces of information with 'It pop up' and 'My mother got peanut butter', she uses her 'playground' dialect of English. Those utterances are accepted by the teacher, but Mary is sensitive to dialect change and switches to 'It's black' after the teacher says 'It's popped up' and she continues in the teacher's dialect with 'It's yucky' and 'It's melting'. She does not need to be taught those standard structures – once a variant has been modelled for meaning and function, she can use it for similar purposes. In these circumstances, modelling is effective because the model has full contextual support.

There seems to be no other explanation for the change, from Transcript A to Transcript D, other than differences between concentrated language encounter sessions and 'normal' classroom contexts.

As Gray states, most of the behaviours that cause children like Mary to be labelled as being in some way different from the majority,

> result largely from confusion about what is required from them in the learning task, their low self-esteem as learners, and experiences of the world that do not lead them to the preconceptions necessary for learning . . . in the manner often taught in schools. (Gray, 1980, 1:3)

They cannot join in classroom learning/teaching processes because they just do not understand what is going on or why.

Whether in the developed or developing world, there are children like Mary wherever there are schools. They may not be Aboriginal, and they may not even be in the minority – one has only to visit schools in almost any developing country to realize that this phenomenon of exclusion from classroom learning exists on a gigantic scale.

With children who, like Mary, speak a first language that differs from the language of instruction, a particularly effective recipe for wholesale failure is to allow only teacher-directed language interaction within the classroom, and to 'cover' only the language elements and structures that are set down in some text book, to be drilled. And in some countries, that is the case across whole regions. Literacy teaching in those places begins with the alphabet, phonic drills, individual words and grammatical rules, and reading and writing for useful purposes is postponed. A whole generation of children find themselves expected to engage, for month after month, in puzzling activities that have no apparent purpose – and before long, they give up trying.

Direct teaching of language also discourages students from learning outside the formal lessons – they learn to learn only when and as directed by a teacher. When each student in a class of thirty or forty has only a few turns in the teacher-directed interaction each day, the quantity and scope of their language experience in school is minimal.

The origins of CLE techniques of teaching

Mary was one of the first group of Aboriginal children to benefit from CLE techniques for literacy teaching. Gray and his colleagues at Traeger Park School worked out classroom learning/teaching contexts that would involve all of a group of children in what was going on, and, within that context, they developed activities from which students learnt to read, write and talk in English, while gaining non-language skills and knowledge that had worthwhile applications in real life.

Over a period of some five years, Gray and his colleagues developed a programme for the early grades of the school in which virtually all the students who attended with anything like reasonable regularity became enthusiastic readers and writers – and there was marked improvement in school attendance.

CLE techniques were introduced into Thailand in 1984 from the Brisbane College of Advanced Education (Rattanavich and Walker, 1990). Chapter 6 relates how those techniques were refined and extended to develop a Thai-language programme and implement it in a large number of primary schools in rural provinces of north-east Thailand.

The programme was next implemented in demonstration schools in the southern border provinces of Thailand, where the mother tongue is a Malaysian dialect, and in the northern provinces, where different hill-tribe languages and dialects are spoken. Then, in 1990, the Thai Ministry of Education announced the adoption of CLE language and literacy teaching principles nationwide, as part of the National Plan for 1992–96.

During 1991, CLE demonstration schools were set up in the remaining parts of the nation, in preparation for implementing the 1992–96 National Plan.

CLE techniques were also taken from Thailand to the Indian subcontinent, where a demonstration programme was set up near Hugli, in India and a successful programme in the Bangla language was piloted in several schools near Dhaka, Bangladesh.

Finally, the movement of CLE techniques from language to language came back to the language in which it began, when work commenced, in Thailand, on a CLE programme for teaching English as a second language.

Conclusion

CLE literacy teaching techniques have proved to be effective in involving all children in learning to read, not just those whose home and cultural backgrounds suit the programmes and teaching techniques that are currently being used in schools. And on the basis of their experience with eradicating gross literacy failure rates in a range of educationally difficult circumstances, the authors contend that the problem lies not so much with the family and ethnic background of the children as with the school literacy programme, and, in particular, with the dynamics of classroom interaction.

Chapter 2 presents a description of CLE teaching techniques in Thai primary schools, Chapter 3 is directed at helping readers to visualize how CLE teachers and their students operate within their classrooms, and Chapter 4 describes the process of developing a CLE literacy programme for primary schools.

Chapters 5 and 6 are an account by Dr John Oller Jr of literacy testing. After reviewing the theoretical position that all three authors agree is basic to learning, teaching and testing literacy, Oller states, in Chapter 5, the basic principles that should be followed in testing. Then, in Chapter 6, he exemplifies those principles, and provides guidelines for a testing programme in literacy.

In view of the imperative need for a new approach to teaching literacy that exists in developing countries that are faced with mass literacy problems, Chapter 6 explains the strategies by which large-scale changes in literacy teaching policy and practice have been achieved in one developing country – Thailand.

In Chapter 7, Richard Walker reflects on some of the issues and insights that arise from what has been presented in the book, and on their significance in understanding what is involved in learning and teaching literacy.

Notes

1. For Australia, see Wickert (1989).

Concentrated language encounter teaching techniques

SAOWALAK RATTANAVICH

Introduction

The term 'concentrated language encounters' has been borrowed from
Courtney Cazden, who made the point (Cazden, 1977) that children learn
language mainly through encounters with others in which the children
concentrate intensely on making themselves understood. As he worked
with Aboriginal students at Traeger Park School, Gray (1983) noted that
the most successful teaching sessions were those in which students were put
in situations where they were doing interesting and useful things, but
where they had to confront challenging language tasks to achieve those
things. This feature underlies all CLE programmes.

A second underlying feature of CLE teaching is 'scaffolding'. The
more that what is said relates to and is supported by the context – the other
things that are happening, the actions, the gestures and tone of voice of the
speakers, and what previous experience the listener has had with all of
these – the easier it is to understand what is being said. In the case of
language learning, the easier it will be to participate in the language interaction, and so to learn from it. This applies also to written language, and
learning written language, but in this case there can be an additional
component to scaffolding, if the learners can already speak the language,
in spoken discourse that is related to or even identical to the written
discourse. As Oller states in Chapter 5,

> the already established connection between utterances in a particular lan-
> guage, and the facts of experience . . . will similarly help the pre-literate child
> to begin to become literate. (p. 58–9)

This chapter presents a description of CLE teaching separately for three
'stages' of primary schooling – the lower, the middle and the upper
grades.

Yet, language learning does not occur in distinct stages – precursors of what becomes predominant in later years are present at earlier stages. So the three stages of the programme are not meant to be rigidly compart-mentalized and students who are rapid learners sometimes engage in learning activities that others do not encounter until a later stage of the programme.

Stage 1 of the programme: The lower primary school grades

The overall teaching objective for Stage 1 of a CLE programme is for beginning school students to become enthusiastic readers and writers. At the end of Stage 1, they should be able to read various types of simple texts, and to recall and talk about what is contained in the texts that they read. They should be able to write several kinds of brief texts, observing the conventions of written language. In progressing to that stage, they will have learned to identify, write and spell hundreds of words from their reading and writing, and to bring effective strategies to bear in recognizing and writing words that they have not previously encountered.

A Stage 1 CLE programme usually covers two or three years, depend-ing on whether or not it is used in preschool or kindergarten classes. The programme for each school year is organized into units, each one extend-ing over a number of weeks. For reasons that will be explained later in this chapter, the actual number of units that are covered in a year will vary from class to class, but most Stage 1 classes in Thailand cover ten to fifteen units in a school year.

Within each Stage 1 programme unit, the teacher and students work through five 'phases', in a fixed sequence. Because there are two kinds of Stage 1 programme units, there are two types of Stage 1 teaching sequence, both of which are illustrated in Fig. 2.1. 'Text-based' units start with the shared reading of a starter book and 'activity-based' units begin with a shared experience of some other kind, such as the toast-making session of Mary's Transcript C in Chapter 1.

Other activities in the north-east Thailand programme are making a paper hat, learning to preserve beans, and breeding fish. In published CLE programmes, a 'How To' (procedure genre, see pp. 46–9, where genre is explained in detail) starter book is provided for some activity-based units but the starter book is only a reference book, and a unit might just as easily begin with a practical demonstration by the teacher or a visiting expert.

As can be seen from Fig. 2.1, Phases 3, 4 and 5 are similar for both kinds of programme units.

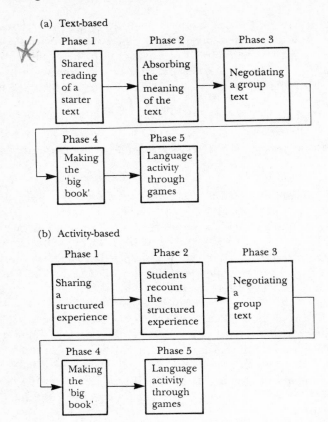

Figure 2.1: Types of Stage 1 CLE units

Phase 1 of an activity-based unit: sharing the experience

In Phase 1 of activity-based units, the teacher demonstrates an activity such as making bread or growing some kind of vegetable. The demonstration can be divided into several sections:

1. discussing what will happen;
2. showing students what materials and equipment are needed;
3. demonstrating, while showing clearly the steps by which the task is carried out; and
4. the students sharing in the activity with the teacher or performing it for themselves.

The teacher and students talk about what they are doing as they do it.

That talk is structured, not in accordance with what is laid down in a programme text, but in accordance with the structure of what is going on: purposeful processes invariably proceed through a series of steps that must occur in a fixed sequence. That being so, the talk that occurs between those who are cooperating in getting the task successfully completed will be structured around and scaffolded by an awareness of those steps. In this case, the children and teacher talk about each step in the process of making toast – what is done, what is used to do it, who are involved in the doing, and how they feel about those things.

Phase 2 of an activity-based unit: reconstructing the experience

Phase 2 is similar for both kinds of programme units in that it concentrates on meaning and recall. In activity-based units, the students list the equipment and materials that are required and tell how to do or make the thing, step by step.

As the students recount a shared activity on repeated occasions, the talk can easily be varied. For example, the teacher can direct attention to different elements of what is going on or the talk can change from simple commentary with action, such as 'I'm planting the bean seeds', while doing that, to more complex language tasks, such as telling what will happen next, what happened to the seed as the days passed, or whether or not something was done properly. Those tasks differ in that they call for different kinds of spoken texts: commentary along with on-going action, a procedural text, a recount text, and a report text, respectively.

Then, as discussed in Chapter 7, the difficulty of the language demand can systematically be increased by gradually separating the talk from the non-language activity and context. Discussion of the activity continues until the students feel that they have expert knowledge of the activity and can confidently talk about it. They are then ready to move across from the spoken to the written language mode in Phase 3, the scaffolds all being in place for written discourse.

Phases 3, 4 and 5 are similar for both types of programme units, but we should first look at Phases 1 and 2 of text-based programme units, as they are shown in Fig. 2.1.

Phase 1 of a text-based unit: shared reading

When the sequence begins with shared reading, the objective in Phase 1 is to have the learners come to a firm understanding of the starter text, from its overall structure down to elements such as what happened, who did what, and the characteristics of people, objects, and events.

The reading should be a leisurely, informal process that involves talking about what is being read, much as parents read a story to their infant children. Teachers bring the whole range of story-telling techniques to bear to make the reading a more exciting and lively experience and, when there are children whose first language is different from the language of instruction, the teacher scaffolds the language in every possible way such as by using pictures from the text, gesturing and using facial expressions. In extreme cases, the teacher may explain essential concepts in the children's first language, though the reading must not become a translation.

However, the substance of the talk, and to a large extent the language needed to talk, have to be supplied and modelled in the shared experience of the reading until at least the more outgoing and confident students, and later the others, can talk with the teacher about what is being read.

Between readings, songs and dances on the same theme can also help children to understand, remember and enjoy the story.

Teachers should be patient with the less confident students, giving them praise for non-language involvement, and waiting for their confidence to build up to the point where they can join in the talk. Once that occurs, they will have permanently left their most serious difficulty behind them.

Phase 2 of a text-based unit: absorbing the meaning of the text

In Phase 2, the main objective is to have the learners recall what they have heard during the Phase 1 readings, making sure that they understand the meaning of what was read.

Phase 2 can follow directly after Phase 1. If not, teachers usually begin by 'warming up' their students with a few simple questions about the story, such as 'What people are in the story?' and 'What happened to (a character)?' The song or dance that was learnt during Phase 1 may also be used in the 'warm up'. The teacher then asks students to retell the story, step by step.

As many students as possible are brought into retelling the story and, at intervals, a student may be allowed to read parts of the book, along with the teacher – perhaps by taking the part of narrator in role-play. But the students should not be made to feel that they have to learn to read or recite the starter book.

When the story has been retold once or twice, role-play is recommended as a means of involving all of the students in recalling the story and in using the language in which it can be told.

The importance of role-play, like some of the other CLE processes, varies according to whether or not the children are operating in their first language. With those for whom the language or dialect is unfamiliar, it provides repeated but enjoyable opportunities to hear the language along with seeing the actual characters and events that the language refers to. If, at first, students are reluctant to role-play individually, several children can role-play the one part, as a group, until one of them becomes confident enough to act alone. Through watching others role-play, shy students develop a sense of participation that usually leads to being able to follow their example. The teacher acts as director of the role-play, helping both the narrators and the players to perform their roles and speak their 'lines' as dramatically as can be. In the next performance, the groups exchange their tasks, the narrators being actors and the actors becoming the narrating group.

Phase 3 of both text-based and experience-based units:
negotiating a group text

During Phases 1 and 2 of a text-based unit, the students absorb the meaning of the story, they then build up an enriched background to the elements and aspects of that story, and, through their own creative thought, they elaborate on what was contained in the story book. By the end of Phase 2, they are able to draw on shared language and experiential resources to tell and talk about their own version of the story. In Phases 1 and 2 of an experience-based unit, the students will have reached a similar stage of being able to recount and talk about the structured experience that they have shared with their teacher and fellow students. In either case, they are now ready to build a written text that conveys what they want to say about what they have read or experienced together.

This first experience focuses primarily on a whole text, not just small elements of it. The teacher asks the students to tell the story or recount the experience again, so that the group can write a book for themselves. She again asks such questions as 'What happened first?', 'Then what happened?' and so on, but this time she writes each sentence on a large sheet of paper, transforming it from the spoken to the written form, before their eyes, to become part of a written text.

Each time she writes a sentence, she will ask the other students if they want to say it a different way and she will change the sentence if another version is preferred. The students thus negotiate an entire written text, sentence by sentence, cooperating to make the text satisfactory in all respects. They read their text many times as it is built up, because the teacher frequently has them chorus read it from the beginning, 'to see what we now have'.

It is preferable to work with groups that are small enough for all the members to make a substantial input to the text, or at least to feel that they have agreed to the wording of all the text. The teacher does not dictate what is written but she modifies sentences as needed to observe accepted language conventions, saying the corrected version as she writes it.

For the first few units of the Stage 1 programme, teachers have to do all the writing. As they write each word, they say it, to enable the students to note the written form of words and parts of words. Some teachers favour having the students chorus the words as they are being written. Later, students will take pleasure in displaying their ability to 'be the teacher' and do some of the writing. For example, they will be able to insert punctuation and (in Thai) tone marks, from a very early stage.

The pages used for writing group texts should be large enough for students to see individual symbols clearly, to chorus read from it, and to check the accuracy of a reading by another student. Spaces are usually left for art work and students draw illustrations at suitable points on each page. To do this, they have to read and think about the overall meaning of that section of the group text.

The negotiating of a group text will not be finished at the one session so it is left in place between sessions, allowing students to read and discuss it at leisure. Before they start work on it again as a group, they chorus read through what has been written, with the teacher pointing to each word as it is read. Again, a student can soon be asked to 'be teacher' and do the pointing as the others read. When the complete text has been written up, teacher and learners go through it together again, discussing whether it can be improved.

If the teacher has proceeded patiently and carefully in negotiating the text with the students, most of them will be able to read the whole text, and to identify any particular word by 'reading up to it'.

Phase 4: making the 'big book'

Then a 'fair copy' is made of the negotiated text, to constitute a 'big book'. After the students have learnt to work in small groups, there can be as many big books made as there will be activity groups in Phase 5. A book that is to be used with the class as one group needs to be as large as a poster or chart. Books for use with smaller groups may be only a quarter of that size.

In some parts of Thailand, the big book was no more than sheets of paper stapled together. At Traeger Park School, elaborate hard-covered big books of intriguing shapes were made. What form the big book takes will vary according to the local circumstances.

The procedures used in making the book will also change as students become better acquainted with book-making and can work with minimal supervision. In any case, the first task is to decide on page layout, and illustrations. That process involves reading the text, discussing what should be in the illustrations and where they should be placed on the page.

When the students work in small groups and print the book for themselves, the more able students help those who are struggling to read the text, so that all can share in the decision-making. The teacher will have prepared for this, while the students were still working in one large group, by modelling helping behaviour and then having prospective leaders 'be teacher'.

To watch students at work in small groups, making their big books, reveals much about their ability to read and write. It is particularly important to monitor how the groups go about editing their book, so that they develop habits of systematic and effective proofreading and self-evaluation.

Phase 5: language games and other group activities

By the time a group of learners have produced their own book, they will be able to chorus read it with ease and most will be able to read it individually, with minimum prompting. As a group exercise, they will be able to identify any word within its context, by 'chorus reading' up to it and they can be brought to do that individually. Some will already be able to identify some of the words in isolation. Most importantly, all will have a firm grasp of the meaning of the text, from its overall structure down to sentences and individual words.

The book now becomes a resource for language activities in which students focus on the smaller elements of the written language, such as sentences, words, letters and phonic correspondences, and sub-skills such as spelling, and parsing. But, as John Oller emphasizes in Chapter 5, behind that, there is always the context of the whole group text and what it represents.

Language games are a way of practising language skills, and of drawing attention to language items and features, without boredom. As a new activity or game is introduced, the students are first trained to take part in the activity and then to manage it by themselves, in small groups.

Teachers take a number of factors into account in deciding what activities to introduce in Phase 5. Level of enjoyment is important, because students learn much faster if they enjoy the games sufficiently to play them in their own time. Secondly, the activities must cover the necessary range of objectives for the unit. Table 2.1 shows the kind of spread that teachers aim for in later units of Stage 1 Thai-language CLE programmes.

Table 2.1　Sample activities for Stage 1, Phase 5

---

1. *Recognizing words that occur in the group big book:* word card games, such as match-word, bingo, domino, word hunt.
2. *Reading sentences that contain words from the big book:* reading competition games, such as word-matching, pair work, fill in the word.
3. *Writing the words that occur in the big book:* playing competitive games, such as hang man, and dictation competition.
4. *Making up sentences, orally, that include words from the book:* sentence-making competition, a sentence for a picture.
5. *Reading and writing sentences that include words from the book:* reading competition, dictation, pair work in reading and writing sentences.
6. *Spelling words from the book, and making up new words:* crossword puzzle, complete the sentence, homonyms, look-a-like words.
7. *Making up sentences, orally, with new words:* shopping game competition – each group prepares a 'shopping list' of words they can put into sentences, and challenge another group.
8. *Reading and writing new sentences:* jigsaw puzzle, of sentences, pair-work or inter-group competition in dictation, small book writing competition.
9. *Reading new texts:* guessing words or sentences from reading competition – prose or poetry.
10. *Recounting or telling the content of a text from everyday life:* 'interviewing a star' game, telephone conversation, twenty questions, charades.
11. *Responding to new texts:* telling stories, news-reading, master chairman contest, TV announcer contest.
12. *Generating short written texts:* cards for occasions, finish the story, writing competition.

In either type of programme unit, the teacher should not hurry over any of the five phases. Before leaving one phase, the students need to be ready for the demands of the next. For the first few programme units, therefore, progress may seem slow but students are able to move faster as they become accustomed to and understand what happens in each phase.

That speeding up is reinforced by growth of self-reliance in individual learning tasks. As soon as possible, learners are given tasks which require individual initiative and leadership and, in the activities of Phase 5, they learn how to solve for themselves most of the problems they encounter.

Stage 2 of the programme: The middle primary school grades

There are many kinds of texts, each with a different characteristic structure (generic structure). Different kinds of texts are written and read for different purposes and need to be written and read in different ways. The

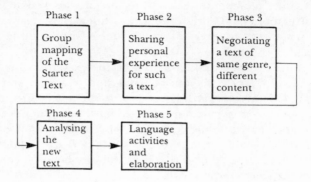

Figure 2.2: CLE unit structures for Stage 2

range of genres encountered in Stage 1 of the programme is necessarily limited so that the central objective at Stage 2 is to widen the students' experience with different kinds of texts (genres), particularly those that are most commonly encountered in everyday life.

In Thailand, starter books are still used in Stage 2. Most of them are examples of one kind of text, such as an instruction manual or a story book but some are collections of different kinds of texts. For example, the one starter book might contain application forms, timetables, posters, letters, invoices, receipts and the like, that are used in everyday life. The Thai starter books for Stage 2 are much larger and have larger print than normal books, to allow the teacher to use them with the whole class as one group.

The overall Stage 2 strategy is to have the students analyse the model text, to come to understand its uses and its characteristics, and then to compose and use a text of that kind for themselves. Within each programme unit, they do that for at least one genre.

Again, there are five phases within each programme unit. Fig. 2.2 shows these five phases.

Phase 1: analysing the model text

The first objective in Phase 1 is for the teacher to model and then help students to use the reading strategies that are appropriate for a particular kind of text. At the same time, the students are also forming a basis for organizing their own ideas into a text of that kind and for improving drafts of their own texts.

In the early weeks of the Stage 2 programme, the teacher will need to use scaffolding techniques to lead the students into talking about the text in a structured and insightful way. Strategies that are commonly used to help students to analyse texts include mapping, note-taking and summarizing.

In general, the teacher asks the students to seek out the main idea and supporting detail for each section or paragraph of a text, and asks questions that guide them towards discovering how the text is organized. To do that the teachers need to have a general understanding of the characteristics of the genres that are to be covered within the programme.

The kinds of questions that teachers ask, and that students should learn to ask themselves as they read a text, will vary between genres but, in general, they are open questions such as:

What are the really important points in this text?
What is the main point in that paragraph?
What is the problem that faces these people?
How can (they) solve the problem, do you think?
Is that a good solution? Why?
What caused that to happen?
What resulted from that?
What are the differences between X and Y?

Phase 2: Linking the text to personal experience

The objective in Phase 2 is to stimulate the students to thought and discussion that leads to their identifying something in their own experience that could just as well be expressed in the same kind of text as the one they examined in Phase 1.

Discussion begins with questions such as:

'How about yourself – has something like that ever happened to you? When? What was it?'
'If you were that character, what would you have done?' Why?

These kinds of questions are used to prompt students to bring forward interesting experiences that could appropriately give rise to the kind of text analysed in Phase 1. When that occurs, the shared experiential and language basis for writing texts of this kind is then enlarged and enriched through focused discussion of personal experiences. Readers who are familiar with systemic-functional grammar will realize that the students are substituting a different 'field' component for the context, retaining the same 'tenor' and 'mode' (see Halliday, 1973).

Phase 3: Negotiating a new text

The students now set out to organize and express their own ideas and experience in a text of the same genre as the one that they analysed in Phase 1.

On the first few occasions, the teacher negotiates the text with the whole class in one group, using questions based on the structure that was revealed in analysis of the sample text. The teacher is still modelling and scaffolding, just as in the Stage 1 teaching/learning processes – but she is now modelling the reasoning and decision-making that is involved in producing and polishing a text of this kind.

For the first few programme units, the teacher works with the whole class, but she gradually prepares the students for work in small groups, by introducing such questions as 'What should we ask ourselves next?', and by fostering leadership by the most confident students until they are capable of leading small groups as they conduct their own negotiating of a text.

The whole progression of Phase 3 of Stage 2 is similar to the same phase of Stage 1, except that the negotiating takes place at the level of structure as well as form – direct attention is now being given to the underlying structure of the text, not only to what is being said and how it is being said. The notion of appropriateness of the language for that kind of text, rather than just correctness or attractiveness, also emerges in the discussions.

The ultimate step for Phase 3 is to have the students independently writing their own texts within each of the genres. This will become possible for different students at different times, and it should not be unduly hurried.

Phase 4: Critically analysing the new text

In Phase 4, the students use the procedures that were modelled in Phase 1 to analyse their own text: they determine how the ideas are organized, they examine the language for appropriateness and clarity, and they proofread for accuracy in grammar, spelling and punctuation – always in that order.

Again, the Phase 4 process is modelled and then scaffolded by the teacher with the whole class before it is controlled by student leaders of small groups. And again, the ultimate aim is to have students take individual responsibility for analysing and improving their own texts, although, for most students, it may not be realistic to expect the latter before Stage 3 of the programme.

Phase 5: Language activities and elaboration

In Phase 5, students are given further opportunities to practise working within the various genres that they have examined to that time. Activities are introduced one by one, until the full range of objectives for this stage of

Table 2.2   Phase 5 activities for Stage 2 of the CLE programme

1. Writing new texts of the same kind as the starter books:
   - writing short texts in a set time;
   - 'Lucky Dip': sketch out a text of the particular genre, with a picture or word as stimulus.
2. Analysing and improving written texts:
   - pair work on student texts;
   - mapping texts in small groups;
   - competition in collecting errors from a set of student texts.
3. Finding texts of the same type as the starter books:
   - competition in finding texts of different types;
   - quiz game on characteristics of different kinds of texts.
4. Writing texts of the same type as the starter books:
   - 'Story-writing' and 'letter-writing' contests.
5. Analysing and improving texts of the same type as the starter books:
   - pair work on improving texts;
   - editorial meetings;
   - explaining the main idea and structure of a group text;
   - jig-saw game: reconstituting a text from sentences.
6. Reporting on texts:
   - TV author interview;
   - newscast;
   - board display illustrating different kinds of texts.
7. Grasping the main idea and supporting ideas from new texts:
   - quiz contest, after reading new texts;
   - illustrating the meaning of a text;
   - filling in gaps in a text;
   - supplying missing parts by illustrating.
8. Summarizing texts:
   - taking notes as teacher reads;
   - mapping texts from reading (can be a competition for speed and accuracy).
9. Comparing and contrasting the structure of words and sentences:
   - domino games (for words);
   - finding synonyms and antonyms;
   - replacing words, retaining the same sentence structure;
   - finding sentences with similar structure.
10. Grouping words and phrases by type and structure:
   - hunting for words of one type from dictionary or texts;
   - collecting words of the same part of speech;
   - collecting and grouping clauses of the same tense.

the programme are covered. Table 2.2 shows sets of some of the activities that were suggested by the pilot schools of north-east Thailand.

To mount the Phase 5 activities, supplementary material is needed in all the genres. Some of that material, such as forms and schedules, is readily available from public and commercial sources and many other types of texts may be cut from newspapers and magazines.

A good way of extending first-hand experience with different kinds of texts is to use the present class activity as a basis for writing a number of different kinds of texts. While growing beans, for example the students might: write an account of the project, write an expository text telling how to grow beans, write a personal letter telling about the project, write a fictional narrative with an agricultural setting, keep cultivation, fertilizing and harvesting records for their garden plot, and write a report on vegetable growing in their village. Some teachers have the children assemble an appropriate range of texts for the one activity, to constitute a project folio.

Stage 3 of the programme: the upper primary school grades

The Stage 3 programme is intended to cover the last few years of primary school, and the same methodology could well carry over into secondary school. Literacy teaching does not lessen in importance in these higher grades; indeed, the need to foster effectiveness in and enthusiasm for literacy activities grows in importance with the approach of secondary school or working life.

As students move into higher levels of schooling, and into adult life, they will encounter a wider variety of texts that are directed towards some specific purpose. The prospects that these students will cope successfully with later stages of schooling and with vocational training depend largely on how well they can cope with the range of specialized reading and writing that is involved.

Accordingly, one component of the Stage 3 programme is to broaden further the range of texts that students have learnt to use. The Stage 2 learning/teaching sequence remains appropriate for that component.

An additional dimension of the Stage 3 programme arises from the fact that ability to use written language to generate and structure new knowledge now becomes of major importance, as increasingly, students are expected to learn for themselves. To learn from different kinds of texts, a reader has to be able to bring to bear the appropriate strategy for each particular kind of text. Moreover, because knowledge is arranged, expressed and reported in different ways in different subject fields, students need to learn how to organize knowledge for themselves in ways that are conventional to subject areas.

For that added dimension of the Stage 3 programme, a different learning/teaching sequence is needed to give students experience in:

1. using 'scientific' ways of finding out about a range of subject matter, within their regular school curriculum;
2. reporting what they have found out.

There are six phases within this additional Stage 3 sequence: orientation, reflection, note-taking, synthesis, editing and final copy.

Again, the students first go through the new learning/teaching sequence, under the guidance of the teacher then they do it in small groups and, finally, they learn to work through the sequence unaided, except for group review of what has been achieved. And again, modelling and scaffolding are used to induct students into these new routines.

Phase 1: Orientation

In Phase 1, having been assigned a reading and writing task, the students are asked to survey a relevant text, analyse its content structure, and use the context to work out the meaning of unfamiliar words.

In leading students through this orientation, in the earliest programme units, the teacher may use a chart, or write up the following steps for guidance.

1. Contextualization
In Stages 1 and 2 of the programme, the reading and writing of a text by the students was preceded by either first-hand shared experience or shared exploration of the content and context of a text. In Stage 3, the students are trained to build up for themselves a context for the text that is compatible with that understood by the author. Students need to ask themselves questions such as:

What is this text about?
Why did the author write it?
For what audience was it written and how much did the author expect a reader to know already?
What do I already know about this topic?
What do I know about using this kind of text?

2. Mapping the topic
Having done that, the students will be ready to pool their own knowledge about the topic of the text. Having used mapping strategies for some years now, they should readily be able to discuss and map their ideas.

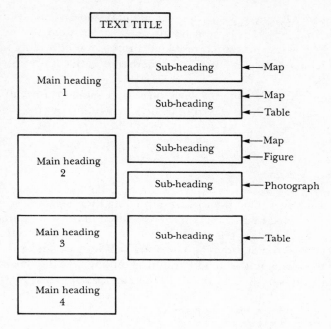

Figure 2.3: A sample graphical outline

3. Surveying the text organization

The students then survey the text for organization of its content, as revealed in headings, sub-headings, illustrations, tables, topic sentences, and summaries.

This survey of the text can result in a graphic outline that predicts the content of the text. A typical graphic outline for a single-chapter text is shown in Fig. 2.3.

4. Establishing the genre of the text being read and the text to be written

From working through Stage 2 of the programme in previous years, the students will readily be able to establish the genre of the text that has been surveyed and remind themselves of the generic characteristics of the text that they are to write.

5. Dealing with unfamiliar vocabulary

The students then deal with unfamiliar vocabulary. There may be words that are unfamiliar because they are part of the technical or semi-technical vocabulary that is associated with the particular topic and genre. There may also be unfamiliar items of general vocabulary.

For the first few programme units, the teacher usually asks the students to locate a few new words, and teacher and students discuss them one by one to decide whether or not the meaning can be worked out from the context, whether the author has provided another way of finding the meaning (such as a glossary or index) or whether it is necessary to consult a reference book.

In later units, the students work on this in small groups, after which the teacher and the whole class discuss how they found out the meaning of unfamiliar words.

Phase 2: Reflection

The students now change their focus to relating their assigned writing task to what is contained in the text that they surveyed in the orientation phase. Their objective at this time is to produce a writing plan from reflecting on both what is required of them in the writing task, and what is available from the text. That plan could well be a graphical outline, like the one in Fig. 2.3 but, this time, it is of the text that they themselves will write.

Table 2.3   Format for a simple writing plan

Introductory paragraph
    Point 1:
    Point 2:
    Point 3:

Paragraph 2
    Major concept:
    Supporting point 1:
    Supporting point 2:
    Supporting point 3

Paragraph 3
    Major concept:
    Supporting point 1:
    Supporting point 2:
    Supporting point 3:

Paragraph 4
    Major concept:
    Supporting point 1:
    Supporting point 2:
    Supporting point 3:

Conclusion
    Point 1:
    Point 2:
    Point 3:

Sometimes, the writing task will be to produce a text of a different genre from the one they have read, in which case their writing plan has to conform to the generic structure that has been specified for them rather than that of the text they have examined.

That writing plan may be a graphical outline, or it may be a simpler construct such as headings and sub-headings. To begin with, the plan may be no more than a simple table, such as that shown in Table 2.3.

The students plan their writing in small groups, which then break up for the individual students to make their own notes for their individual texts, in Phase 3. The teacher does not guide students in this phase unless a difficult new task has been assigned.

When the teacher, or the student group, is satisfied with the writing plans, the students are ready to search out what they need to write a text based on that plan.

Phase 3: Note-taking

The briefing for this step takes place in Phase 2 so that, from the beginning, the students are able to work in small groups for this Phase. Each student fills in an individual writing plan with information that was noted down from reading the text. Then each group reconvenes, to negotiate a common set of notes for the group. The discussion that takes place in this step is among the most highly instructive shared experiences of the Stage 3 CLE processes.

Phase 4: Synthesis

The students now write a first draft of a text that is aimed at realizing the writing task goal.

At first, a group text is written by the negotiating procedures that are familiar from Stages 1 and 2 of the programme. The more capable students may be ready to work alone almost from the beginning, but their presence is valuable in a group that is negotiating a text. Before long, all the students should be able to write their text individually and then come together only to share in a review of their draft texts, in Phase 5. This is a case where a 'small group' may be as small as two students.

In any case, the students are urged, beforehand, to establish:

1. the purposes of the text, and
2. the audience for the text,

and to keep those two firmly in mind as they turn their notes into a continuous text.

Phase 5: Editing

There are three steps for Phase 5: *reviewing, redrafting* and *polishing.*

1. Reviewing

The review is carried out through group discussion and negotiation. The students examine their texts for adequacy and suitability in relation to the task goal. They focus first on whole-text qualities such as completeness, structure and logical progression, and then on appropriateness and accuracy of wording.

2. Redrafting

The students then redraft their texts, in the light of the review. Initially, this involves brain-storming and negotiating, to fill in gaps or improve logical progression, and then rewriting to improve effectiveness and clarity of expression. As the year progresses, students are encouraged to carry out that redrafting step individually, as a conventional step in the authoring process.

3. Polishing

The final step is a thorough polishing of the redraft. For the first few units of the programme, the teacher may lead the whole group in polishing a group text, discussing ways of eliminating surface weaknesses such as errors in grammar, spelling and punctuation. But the students should soon learn to carry them out as a group exercise, and then as an individual exercise.

Phase 6: Final copy and elaboration

Final copy

In this final stage, the students discuss what physical properties are needed for the text to best serve its purposes and they produce a final copy in accordance with their decisions.

The final copy may be made into a book for the classroom or home library, it may be photocopied for distribution to other students, it may be put up on a display board as a poster, and so on, in accordance with the function for which it was designed and written.

Elaboration

In the course of a programme unit, the teacher will have noted that some students or groups of students are having difficulty with a particular process, such as surveying a text or compiling a writing plan and that others are ready to go on to more individualized work.

At the conclusion of this final phase of the unit, the teacher organizes independent activities for groups of students or individuals in some aspect of reading and writing, while she works with those students who need help to strengthen their participation in the next programme unit.

Sets of cloze exercises, semantic mapping exercises, context-clue exercises, jig-saw reading, crossword puzzles, and 'make up the question from the answer' games, are a few of the kinds of activities that strengthen or extend the literacy insights and skills for those involved in a Stage 3 programme. Most modern published programmes have activity books that contain useful ideas for use here. Mount Gravatt Developmental Language Reading Program (BCAE, 1982), and *Learning to Learn from Text* (Morris and Stewart-Dore, 1984) are good examples.

As John Oller states in Chapter 6, exercises like these can be used for evaluation as well as learning, without any change of stance or philosophy. It is in the elaboration step, too, that every student can achieve the reading and writing independence that will be needed in later education or later life. The modelling and scaffolding techniques that persist throughout all levels of the programme, and the progression from class-group, to small-group, to paired and finally to individual learning, support and facilitate the development of independence in reading and writing. Ability to work through a Stage 3 programme unit alone and unaided, is the final goal for every student within the programme and teachers use this final step of each programme unit to monitor and foster the progress of individual students towards that goal.

CLE across the curriculum

Ideally, the Stage 3 programme would spread across all subject areas of the primary school curriculum. However, that possibility is remote when a CLE programme is first introduced and it would probably be unwise, in any case, until teachers are confident of their mastery of the methodology.

In schools where the same person teaches all subjects, the CLE methodology is likely to spread fairly quickly across other subjects. In that case, the students will learn to use the kinds of texts that are used in other school subjects within the time allocated to those subjects. This will allow more room within the language-arts or literacy programme for working with the traditional literary genres.

On the other hand, where students have different teachers for different subject areas in the upper grades, the CLE programme is not likely to spread beyond the 'language' area for some years. This puts pressure on the 'language' programme, because work with all the various kinds of texts has to be done within the time allocated to that strand of the curriculum. It then becomes a priority to introduce the teachers of other subjects to CLE literacy teaching.

It will be obvious from this chapter that CLE teaching necessarily involves fluid classroom groupings. Students sometimes work as a class group, sometimes in a number of small groups, and at other times individually, with changes from one to another often occurring within the one session. For that reason, it has been found that teachers who are accustomed only to teaching their class as one group need to learn new classroom management strategies. This is the topic of Chapter 3.

Classroom management

SAOWALAK RATTANAVICH

Introduction

In traditional classrooms, the interaction between teacher and students is teacher-dominated, virtually all interaction is between the teacher and one child (or a group of children who must answer as one), and the normal procedure is for the teacher to initiate each instance of interaction and then to indicate which child is to respond. Deliberate abandonment by the teacher of domination of the classroom language interaction represents a fundamental change in the teacher's classroom role, requiring a different kind of classroom management. But that is only one difference between a classroom that is managed by a CLE teacher and other, more traditional classrooms. Table 3.1 lists the differences between the CLE and the traditional classroom.

These characteristics of a CLE classroom cannot be brought about without planning and careful management. In the description of CLE teaching techniques in Chapter 2, mention was made of strategies by which some of those changes can be instigated. For example, it was frequently stated that some particular activity is first carried out by the whole class group, under the control of the teacher, and then by small groups each led by a student who has been trained to lead. This chapter presents a more complete and methodical explanation of strategies for managing a CLE classroom.

Rationale

There are compelling reasons for changing the perceived source of motivation and control from the teacher to purposes to do with what students are trying to achieve. The speed with which young children learn to speak their

Table 3.1   A comparison between CLE and traditional classrooms

CLE classroom	Traditional classroom
The activities	
Student activities are always related to real-life contexts that have importance to the learners.	The lesson content is usually based on language units, rules and structures.
Students are encouraged to work independently.	Students generally do only what the teacher tells them to do.
Games and songs are used to enliven learning.	Usually not found in the traditional classroom.
Students often read and play language learning games in free time.	Students seldom read or write outside class lessons.
Classroom interaction	
Students learn by interacting among themselves and with the teacher.	The teacher asks questions and selects those who should answer.
There is a great deal of negotiating of meaning by students, with teacher as moderator.	The teacher acts as broker and the students merely receive information, often passively.
The pace of learning is not prescribed. Students can participate in the learning activities, whatever their stage of learning.	A fixed amount of learning is prescribed for each particular period of time.
Classroom management	
Learners often work in small groups, actively discussing and cooperating.	The students usually work seated in rows as a class group, stationary.
Students frequently manage their own activities.	Students await direction from the teacher before speaking or acting.
Discipline is positive. Students are work-oriented.	Discipline is negative. Students are kept under control by prohibitions.
Student attitudes	
Students assume responsibility, with self-confidence and self-actualization. Student leadership is systematically developed and used.	Many of the learners do not participate in learning. They are inclined to lack confidence when asked to communicate.

first language is matched by the earnestness and persistence that they bring to the task. They are prepared to go on trying to use language because they want to get things done. They often take the initiative, and they sometimes persist in trying to make themselves understood in the face of repeated failure.

Similarly, rapid literacy learning occurs when students are enthusiastically and constantly engaged in purposeful activities to do with reading and writing. The success of CLE literacy teaching depends on maintaining that kind of situation within classrooms and the teachers who are most successful with CLE teaching invariably are those who are most adept at managing CLE classroom routines in such a way that all the students enthusiastically participate. That represents a challenge for teachers who have worked only in conventional classrooms, because a different kind of relationship is needed between them and their pupils to achieve maximal conditions for rapid learning.

Management objectives

Within CLE classrooms, there are objectives operating at several levels. Hopefully, all the students and teachers share the common objective of succeeding in the task at hand, whether it be the production of a group big book or the growing of the finest crop of beans in the province. Students are also motivated by personal objectives such as the joy of achievement and the teacher has objectives, to do with the educational process, that are not usually shared by the students.

One important teacher objective is that the learning/teaching activities continue to a successful conclusion, through all the phases of the programme unit, and that they do not break down. Every other aspect of classroom management is subsidiary to this. Experienced CLE teachers work gradually towards having more and more students share that focus, by systematically training their students to participate in each kind of CLE learning/teaching routine and, finally, to manage routines for themselves.

That is not to say that disorder is tolerated for fear of interruption to the learning/teaching sequence. Because CLE activities are directed at practical outcomes that are known and valued by the students, they tend to favour behaviour that contributes to achievement of that purpose and to reject anything that does not. Order is maintained because disorder interferes with prospects of success in the shared activity. Industry and order in the classroom no longer depend on the presence and will of a teacher, alone.

A second concern of a CLE teacher is that all the students participate in the learning activities as often and as continuously as possible, on the reasonable assumption that the more often and more intensely a student is involved, the more rapidly he/she will learn. If the class always works in one large group, not every student can be given an active role in what goes on. The way to bring about maximum student involvement is to have the students working in small groups, in pairs, or, ultimately, as individuals.

These conditions can be achieved only through systematically training the students to work in small groups, and to take more and more responsibility for managing their own group work.

CLE classroom management is facilitated by the fact that the phase structure of programme units remains constant through each of the three stages of the programme. This means that the overall classroom routine becomes increasingly familiar to the students and the teacher needs to devote progressively less time and attention to helping students to participate.

A third objective of CLE classroom management is to foster student personal characteristics such as self-confidence and a willingness to take risks in mastering a new literacy skill. Cooperative attitudes, a willingness to negotiate with others for a better result, and to perceive where there is room for improvement in their own performance, are also fostered. Students develop leadership skills and gain self-confidence through learning to lead a small work group and students learn to get along with others, and to contribute to group decision-making while they are pursuing, with others, the common purpose of writing a group book, for example.

Finally, when most or all of the students are from non-literate families, as is often the case in educationally difficult places, there is a particular need for them to become immersed in book-reading, book-writing and book-making at school.

Keeping all the students actively involved, managing a number of small groups instead of the one class group, encouraging students to cooperate with others and to undertake more and more active and challenging roles within the groups, require classroom management that is characteristically different from that of teacher-dominated classrooms. The remainder of this chapter presents suggestions and ideas for achieving the appropriate kind of classroom management for CLE teaching.

General management techniques

Classroom organization

The most fundamental requirement is that the classroom itself allows for flexibility in student grouping. For sessions in which the teacher models literacy behaviour, or takes the students through a new routine, the children will need to be clustered in the one large group. At other times, the requirement will be for a number of groups of four or five students, working independently. And sometimes, students have to carry out individual tasks, even at the same time as small groups are working.

For Stages 1 and 2, it has been found that a classroom needs to have the following:

1. A clear floor space wide enough for the whole class to sit in a semi-circle for shared reading, negotiating a text, and conference sessions between the teacher and the whole class. That area should be left permanently clear, to allow the teacher to call the whole class together at any time.
2. Clusters of desks or tables that will allow four or five students to work together, or, alternatively, this area can be used for individual work that needs seating or a flat surface.
3. An area for storage of language games and supplementary reading materials. It can also serve as a display and storage area for group big books and word cards. The big books can be placed on display shelves, hung over racks or clamped on to rails along a wall.
4. A quiet reading corner, near the supplementary reading materials.
5. A corner for storage of writing and book-making materials.
6. A wall area with display boards for individual student work, posters and charts that are generated within the literacy programme.

The composition of student work groups

By and large, each small group should contain students with different ability levels. That reflects normal social life and it allows for desirable and productive social behaviours such as helping one another, and taking pride in a personal contribution to a common task while also respecting every other person's contribution. Students will inevitably realize that some of them learn more quickly and easily than others, but they will not feel labelled as they would be if they worked in homogeneous ability groups. Moreover, mixed ability groups present the more able students with the challenge and opportunity of leading the group, as a whole, to a higher level of achievement and satisfaction through more effective cooperation and communication.

It is advisable, too, to change the composition of work groups for different tasks or for different phases of the programme unit, so that students will be given the opportunity to interact with and learn to relate to all of their fellow students. Furthermore, a student who cannot be given a turn as a leader in one group may have a turn at being leader in another.

Flexibility of time limits

Different classes and different class groups will work at somewhat different speeds and, in particular, one group may become particularly enthused with different programme units. Whether the work is being done by the whole class, a small group or by individuals, the students should not be prevented from completing their task to their own satisfaction, because of the importance of generating a sense of responsibility for the quality of their own work. Moreover, the success of the next phase of a programme unit very often rests on the soundness and completeness of what was done in the previous phase. Consequently, rigid time limits should not be imposed on a programme unit or on individual phases of a programme unit.

Moreover, the nature of a CLE programme unit allows for recursion, in that, after generating and using one kind of text, a class group may go back to Phase 3 and generate a second or even a third text, perhaps of different kinds. Consequently, within sensible limits, each class should move through a programme unit at the pace that suits the students and their stage of learning. Within a school year, different class groups may be given equivalent sets of experiences and achieve equivalent gains in literacy learning from a very different number of programme units.

Providing individualized instruction

Within the same class, too, one small group may work at a different speed from another but all should be allowed to complete their task at their own pace. That will require some groups to elaborate their task, or to engage in extension activities of some kind, until other groups are ready to go on to the next phase of the work. That requires teacher ingenuity, but student groups will not remain goal-oriented and self-motivated if the teacher imposes arbitrary limits on what can be achieved. Of course, teachers can unobtrusively give special support to a slow group, and assist them to succeed more quickly. A group that achieves its goals, but at a slower pace, is likely to aim at achieving its next set of goals at a faster pace. Whereas one that is prevented from achieving its goals is likely to be discouraged by failure.

In every class, too, there are differences between individual students in general ability and in progress in learning to read and write. The teacher should be the one who is most aware of those differences, so that she will be ready to assist any student who is having real difficulty. One of the principles of CLE teaching is to have students solve their own problems but they need to be shown how to do that and, above all, they must build up confidence that they can succeed. For that to be the case, the teacher needs to be alert to instances in which students of lower ability are faced with possible failure, and to provide whatever support the student needs to struggle through to a solution of the problem.

That is much easier to do when other students can work in independent small groups. While other groups carry on with their tasks, the teacher can join a group that is having trouble and she can prevent the occurrence of difficulties for individual students by helping them with appropriate scaffolding. An important part of literacy learning is learning how to solve problems.

It is not usually necessary to form special remedial groups within a CLE programme. Nor has it been found necessary to devise a special programme for very able students. In a programme where students generate, illustrate and use texts of various kinds, there is no limit to the difficulty of the tasks that able students can attempt. They can pursue those challenges to whatever level of excellence, while the teacher helps other students to consolidate and strengthen their grasp of what they have learnt to do to that time.

A balance should be kept, for able students, between working on challenging tasks and helping others to solve less difficult problems. And teachers should remember that their very able students will also need individual attention and assistance to achieve what they are capable of. Sometimes all that is needed is to note and appreciate what these students have achieved. At other times, they may need to share their thoughts on some original project they want to undertake or on aspects of language that have not yet interested the other students.

Trends in class management

CLE classroom management should never be static – it should develop throughout each year and from year to year. That development becomes possible because of the additional things that students learn to do: they learn to participate successfully in more demanding types of classroom procedures, and to take greater responsibility for their own learning so that management techniques that require more of the students' initiative and self-reliance may be introduced. Of course, teachers need to train their students to undertake and participate in each new routine, as part of their classroom management.

In respect to basic classroom routines, development can occur on the following dimensions.

1. Greater demands can progressively be made on the students for participation in existing CLE routines.
2. As management problems diminish with greater student mastery of existing CLE routines, further, more demanding types of routines may be introduced.
3. Students will learn to act as leader of a CLE activity group, thus freeing the teacher to help other sub-groups.

4. The students will progressively be expected to solve more and more of their own problems, and make more of their own decisions.

Teachers should ensure that students come to understand what is required of them, within every new type of learning activity, and help them to take control over the activity until, eventually, they can carry it out unsupervised. That is a central principle of CLE classroom management, because it is essential to producing students who are independent readers and writers and who will improve their literacy through independent learning, outside school and beyond their school years.

Classroom management for Stage 1

General principles

1. Begin with sound training in the basic CLE routines and systematically add to the number and variety of routines, unit after unit.
2. At the beginning, work with the one large group but train a few confident students to lead small groups in an activity that they have learnt with you.
3. Begin small group work with one activity at a time then work towards having several groups working simultaneously on different tasks.

Working with texts

1. Begin by negotiating one text with the whole class, work towards having small groups negotiate their own texts, and, finally, individual students will write short texts for themselves.
2. Not all texts need be made into books of the conventional type, sheets of paper can be collated to make chart-like books.
3. Progressively increase the variety of the book formats, types of illustrations, and types of script.

Classroom management for Stage 2

General principles

Accustom the students to a classroom procedure based on the following steps:

1. a briefing by the teacher on what is to be done and how;

2. the students work on the task, in small groups;
3. the class reassembles to review the work, with the teacher leading.

As the students master the demands of this routine, work gradually towards:

1. having students take individual responsibility for part of the group task and;
2. having a group of students review their work, for themselves, before the teacher conducts a review.

Working with texts

1. At this stage, the students will work with many non-literary texts, such as brochures, instruction manuals, telephone books, commercial and public documents, and notices and advertisements. These should be used, where possible, as part of a real project.
2. Only special, selected texts will be made into books of the conventional type.
3. Instead of negotiating the wording of texts, the group will very often negotiate change on one dimension of an existing text (e.g. use an owner-manual for a camera as a model for writing an owner-manual for a cassette player or change a report on growing mushrooms into an instruction manual for growing mushrooms).

Overall

1. Move always towards self-reliance and independence in learning. For that to happen, students must be shown how to overcome their own difficulties, while learning.
2. Strive to have every student continually thinking about or participating in the work.

Classroom management for Stage 3

Organization

Accustom the students to an additional learning routine which follows the following steps:

1. identification of a problem or task;

2. a conference to decide on how to solve the problem or carry out the task;
2. individual effort towards fulfilling the requirements of the task;
4. review of the outcomes.

As the students progress through these final years, work towards the more strictly scientific process:

'analysis of problem → solution → evaluation
of outcome → further response'

Working with texts

1. Students will usually work alone with a text but use paired-learning where appropriate.
2. One major emphasis in reading will be on learning from texts.
3. In writing, the students will discuss the structure of the text – with reference to task requirements – before they work on the wording.
4. The other major emphasis, will be on reviewing texts. This should involve thinking and talking about texts, thinking about the processes involved in reading and writing, finding out about the public uses of various kinds of texts, and discussing how to improve the effectiveness of functional texts.

Summary

The simplicity of the structure of CLE programme units and the use of many well-known teaching techniques can mislead casual observers. The differences between CLE and most other teaching methodologies lie deeper than what casual observation of a CLE classroom will reveal. At the level of classroom dynamics, of development within each programme unit, and of teacher–student interaction, the CLE teaching techniques that are described in Chapter 2 represent a fundamental change from what happens in most conventional classrooms, and their success requires a very different type of learning environment.

Not all of that difference can be described in terms of what a classroom looks like or what is done within it. The most significant differences are attitudinal, with enthusiasm replacing boredom, and with happy and purposeful activity replacing the apathy of hopelessness.

Moreover, there is not just one type of CLE classroom management. The nature of the classroom as a learning environment, and therefore the

LEEDS METROPOLITAN UNIVERSITY LIBRARY

role of the teacher as classroom manager, changes from one stage of the programme to the next.

In Stage 1, while the emphasis is on deriving sound basic understandings about reading, writing and written language, the classroom is primarily an activity centre, where students participate in group and individual literacy activities.

In Stage 2, where there is a widening of experience with texts and with reading and writing texts differently for different purposes, the classroom is primarily a workshop, where students get things done.

In Stage 3, the classroom may be seen as primarily a laboratory for life, where students learn the literacy skills and procedures that they will need in later life.

That is not to say that Stage 1 students do not 'get things done' as a result of their 'participating', or that Stage 2 students do not learn how to 'seek out information' while they 'get things done'. All three activities: participating, getting things done, seeking out information, are achieved at every stage, but, from stage to stage, there is a change of emphasis and that change of emphasis necessitates a change in how teachers manage their classrooms.

In Chapters 2 and 3, we examined CLE teaching and the management of CLE learning within classrooms. However, a CLE programme needs to be developed where it is to be used and Chapter 4 describes how that may be done.

Developing a CLE primary school literacy programme

RICHARD WALKER

Introduction

To develop a new literacy programme requires time and considerable human and material resources (and, as will be discussed in Chapter 7, those resources are not always readily available in developing countries). Account must be taken, too, of what level of provision is available to continue the programme after it has been implemented. It is not sensible, for example, to set up a highly complex programme in a place where there are few trained teachers, poor technical support or, in a poorly resourced school, to develop a programme that requires large recurrent expenditure.

Even in more affluent places, there is a tendency to underestimate the time, personnel and other resources that are needed to build a literacy programme firmly and well. It takes a year to trial each year of a programme so the minimum time for developing a literacy programme for the primary school is six to eight years.

On the other hand, there is a simplistic view that increased expenditure is all that is needed to alleviate a literacy problem and a complementary view is that a low-cost programme is an inferior one. Neither view is sound. Literacy problems within special situations in affluent communities may prove particularly intractable, for the very reason that elaborate and expensive efforts have already been made to solve them.

The failure of repeated expensive efforts to improve a poor situation brings about the worst kind of hopelessness. In those circumstances, it becomes all the more desirable to develop the programme where it is to be used and to involve those who will use the programme in developing it, from the earliest possible stage. It is probably better not to begin programme development in these kinds of situations until that level of local participation is assured.

Assuming that these kinds of general factors will be taken into account, the remainder of this chapter is devoted to techniques for developing CLE literacy programmes. The same basic principles apply whether the programme be for an industrialized country or for a developing country. However, the scale of operations when the work is in a developing country causes additional difficulties that are covered in Chapter 7.

Programme objectives

The first step in developing a CLE programme, like any other, is to set down its objectives after which comes the task of devising the content and structure of a programme through which those objectives may be achieved.

CLE programmes are not based on objectives to do with lists of language items, functions and structures, or on the development of abilities or skills that are assumed to be involved in reading and writing. Instead the central focus is on the real-life needs of the learners. In respect to literacy, those needs may be stated in terms of the kinds of texts (written genres, see pp. 46–9) that students will need to deal with, and what they will need to be able to do with those texts. In other words, CLE programming is based on the principle that literacy learning is essentially becoming able to read and write more kinds of texts, and to use them more effectively.

Ability to read and write has value not so much in itself as in what it gives access to. Being able to compose effective notices, advertisements, and other persuasive or instructional texts, increase power to influence what others do. Ability to read travel books, history books, science magazines, hobby books, brochures, novels, and poems, to mention just a few, enables people to learn more about and reflect on the world and what goes on within it. And so we could go on across the full range of written genres, showing that learning to use each genre constitutes an increase in power to get things done.

So, programme developers need to decide

1. what kinds of texts (written genres) will be encompassed by each stage of their programme and
2. what students should learn to do with those texts.

Because one of the major reasons for reading and writing texts is to gain knowledge and/or skills, it would be as well to consider, also,

3. what non-language knowledge and skills would be useful to learners at the various stages.

Texts and genres

Following Halliday and Hasan (1985), a text, whether spoken or written, is defined as 'language that is functional': a cohesive body of language that is used to get something done.

There is usually more than one step involved in getting something done, so that most texts have structure. Texts that are oriented towards the same goal, are said to be of the same genre, and they tend to have a similar (generic) structure. Besides the recognized literary genres, there are the spoken and written genres of everyday life, such as letters, speeches, advertisements, service encounters, notices, instruction manuals, and interviews.

The text types that are listed as examples in this chapter are for north-east Thailand and differ somewhat from those for other regions of the country or other countries, because the usefulness of some genres depends on aspects of everyday life. For example, bus and train schedules are included in the Stage 2 curriculum for these north-east provinces, but that is not so for hill-tribe schools in the northern provinces. In contrast, bus schedules would probably be listed for Grade 1 in a school in Bangkok.

What students read and write about (non-language content) also varies from place to place. The procedural texts that are listed for the north-east provinces, for example, deal with how to breed fish, maintain a garden and store drinking water – matters of vital urgency in the dry rural north-east, but of little importance in the wet southern provinces or in Bangkok city.

Overall, it has been found in Thailand that about three-quarters of the starter books are suitable for use in all regions of the country. They are called 'core' starter books to distinguish them from 'regional' starter books that are written for use in some particular part of the country.

In practice, the genre coverage of the programme is not limited by the range of starter books. Rather it depends on what students do within the learning/teaching activities that follow from the starter books because the possibility is there for students to go on to write two or even more different kinds of texts within the one programme unit and Level 1 students, for example, may go on to write letters, advertisements, and other kinds of texts in some of their programme units, in spite of the fact that only story, information and procedural ('How To') starter books are provided at that level.

In Thailand, sufficient starter texts were provided to allow teachers to have some choice, because conditions, and therefore needs, vary there between schools even in the same region. Teachers are encouraged, too, to develop additional programme units that are based on activities of local importance.

One class may read and write the same number of books and cover the same number of genres as another, while working through considerably fewer programme units. That happens when students become exceptionally engrossed in a particular topic and they go on to write several different kinds of texts. CLE literacy programmes are meant to have that kind of flexibility.

Stage 1

In the course of the Stage 1 programme, students usually write and use the following kinds of texts:

1. Story books, such as
   (a) single-episode narratives, telling of legends or carrying a moral and;
   (b) recounts, telling the sequence of events of a student project (e.g. 'Planting Our Rice').
2. Procedural texts (called 'How To' books) such as, 'How To Make a Paper Hat' or 'How to Bottle Beans'.
3. Expository texts (called 'Information Books'):
   (a) descriptions of a place, thing, or people (e.g. 'This is Surin', 'My Home' or 'The Frog Family') and
   (b) books about a class of things (e.g. 'Our Book of Birds').
4. Incidental letters, notices, messages and display texts of various kinds.

Stage 2

By the time students complete Stage 1, they typically have become independent readers and writers of simple texts within some genres and they already have implicit understandings of differences between those kinds of texts. Some of those differences will also have been given incidental explicit attention, but students now deepen and systematize their understandings of the differences between the different types of texts, and how to use texts for different purposes. Accordingly, the starter books for Stage 2 include examples of 'public' texts, such as advertisements and bus timetables, that are used in everyday life, different kinds of letters, and the like, as well as narrative, procedural, and expository texts.

In the genres that are continued from Level 1, the starter texts become more complex and more sophisticated in both structure and content. The following is a general description of that trend for a Stage 2 programme:

1. Stories with a more complex structure than in Stage 1, including:

(a) Longer episodical narratives set in some other time ('Once upon a time . . .') or some other place ('In a far-off country . . .').

(b) Stories with a recountal embedded within them and stories with a recurrent structure (like, 'The Boy Who Cried Wolf').

(c) True narratives (with a setting–complication–resolution structure).

In general, the students progress from writing 'recount' to writing 'reports', and then to true narratives.

2. Procedural and expository books that have practical uses – the focus is on the content – and the students tend to write more than one kind of text in the course of the programme unit.

3. Brochures and pamphlets, are good models for using within the particular community.

4. Letters for personal communication.

5. Newspaper items such as reports of local events, advertisements and cartoons.

6. Verse, jingles, fun with language.

Stage 3

The genres that students deal with in this final stage of elementary schooling encompass as complete a coverage as possible of what they will need in later life. Students who are going on to secondary education should encounter the types of texts that they will be required to study and write at secondary school and all the students should learn to deal with the kinds of texts that they are likely to encounter in private and commercial life.

Level 3 students are concerned with such genres as:

1. newspaper articles and reports;

2. short stories of literary quality (fictional narrative);

3. biographies, travel tales (factual narrative);

4. plays and films;

5. radio scripts (including advertisements);

6. commercial and public documents, such as user manuals, government forms, commercial documents, business letters, invoices, receipts and accounts, timetables, catalogues;

7. reference books, e.g. dictionaries, encyclopaedias.

8. texts used in formal business, minutes of meetings, annual reports of community bodies, and speeches.

In these final years of the elementary school, it is neither possible nor desirable to provide models of some of the genres, such as novels, plays, reference books, application forms, schedules, reports and films within the reading programme itself – examples exist and are used in the wider community or in other subject areas of the school curriculum. But examples can be provided of particularly important types of public and commercial texts and the typical structure for others can be given, for students to use in examining authentic texts, including their own.

In some cases, too, it is not desirable to prescribe additional reading within the literacy programme, because that would tend to be restrictive rather than facilitative. Instead, schools need to widen the range of genres that are available to students in the school library. With classroom reading and writing activities becoming more and more individual, the need for a good school library becomes ever more urgent.

Genres should not be thought of apart from operational and referential context, as those concepts are explained in Chapter 8. A genre is associated with a particular kind of social process and generic structure arises from the nature of that social process. It follows that learning to read and write a particular genre involves learning to read and write appropriately within particular kinds of operational contexts.

Focus

Focus refers to what students will learn to do with the types of texts that are listed for that Stage of the programme.

Stage 1

In the Stage 1 programme, the overt emphasis is on enjoyment from finding meaning and making meaning in print. But the educational purposes include a consolidation and enrichment of basic understandings about reading, writing, and written language as well as a demonstration of the usefulness of reading and writing in enabling people to do interesting, enjoyable and satisfying things. That was the focus of these same children as they set out to learn to speak their mother tongue and the focus must remain the same in their first formal acquaintanceship with written discourse, because we want them to continue to use the same language-learning strategies, with similar enthusiasm and persistence.

Stage 2

In Stage 2, there is a widening of the variety of the texts and the fields of knowledge that they treat, and the focus is on using different reading and writing strategies for different purposes.

Stage 3

In Stage 3, the focus moves to using reading and writing to learn and to cope with demands on their literacy that they will meet in the immediate future.

Non-language content

'Relevancy' is an overused word but it is an important one to keep in mind when framing a reading/writing programme for those who as yet do not see anything like the full extent to which reading and writing can be of value in their daily lives. If the knowledge and skills that students acquire while learning to read and write are immediately useful in their daily lives, they are likely to be convinced of the value of literacy, and their literacy is likely to go on growing and improving, through continued use.

The non-language content of a literacy programme will change, of course, as students move up through the grades. But there should also be differences between programmes for different school populations. What is a valuable piece of knowledge or an essential skill in northern Cornwall may be completely irrelevant in Brixton or Leeds. And what are essential knowledge and skills for children in rural Tennessee may have only curiosity value in down-town Memphis.

Choice of the non-language content of the reading programme is crucially important when, through poverty, people necessarily place a high priority on individual and community welfare and material needs. Anything that is irrelevant to those urgent needs is likely to have a low community priority so that the topics of the reading, writing, and talking should include some that are of high importance to the learners' immediate welfare and happiness. For that reason, at least some of the decisions for content should be made locally.

For the poor rural areas of north-east provinces of Thailand, for example, units of the literacy programme were written around hygiene, immunization against preventable diseases, and clean water storage and where malnutrition is a problem, children are likely to learn how to set up and maintain a school fish and poultry farm, and a vegetable garden, in the course of reading and writing about that. Whether or not students learn how to set up and maintain a fish farm, for example, depends on whether or not one is in operation at their school.

Programme materials

The classroom kit

In the Thai-language CLE programmes, a classroom kit contains the following:

Starter texts for use by the teacher in introducing the programme units. For example, fifteen such texts were supplied in the initial north-east Thailand programme. Students do not read the published starter books. Instead, they 'write' for themselves the group and/or individual texts that they use within the programme.

There is a *teacher's guide* for each stage of the programme, and *teacher's notes* for each programme unit. In Thailand, there are usually two volumes of teacher's notes: one for the core starter texts, and one for the starter texts for the particular region.

The classroom kit also contains *equipment that is needed to teach* that grade level for the first time but is not otherwise likely to be available in a classroom. For Stage 1 classes, that includes a 'pocket' chart, a supply of large sheets of cheap paper, sheets of white card, sets of wick pens, scissors and glue. Most of those are reusable or refillable in subsequent years.

Supplementary reading material is needed for each grade beyond the first, because of the rapid growth of enthusiasm for reading and writing. And children must, of course, handle and use published books, as well as those that they and their fellow students write. In developing countries, that becomes a difficulty, albeit a positive one, because there are seldom adequate school libraries.

Teacher inservice training

The success of programmes as innovative as these depend on effective inservice training of teachers. And in places where there has been long-term serious educational failure, those teachers who will use the programme need to see, first-hand, that the programme will work with students like theirs.

The setting up of 'pilot' schools and classes is a first priority as a CLE programme is developed in a new region, because of the need to trial programme materials as part of the programme developmental process.

The training of teachers is not usually done at the 'pilot' schools nor are 'pilot' classes used to demonstrate the methodology. Instead, the first step towards introducing the programme into a group of schools is to have a member of the CLE programme development team demonstrate each step of a Stage 1 CLE unit, with children from one of the target schools. This is usually done in three or four sessions, over a period of several days.

It has been found that this is a far more effective introduction to the methodology than any amount of talking, showing of videos, slide presentations, and the like. Teachers will see someone else teaching their pupils much more than they themselves could hope to do and, in particular, see students like their own becoming enthusiastically involved in learning.

After such a demonstration, teachers are usually ready to volunteer for a week-long seminar/workshop. They return from that seminar with the materials and information they need to teach several programme units. After the teachers begin to implement the programme, periodic teachers' meetings are held to allow them to discuss problems with members of the CLE project team, and to share ideas and experiences with one another. The more complex procedures that are needed for large-scale programme implementation are discussed in Chapter 7.

Inservice teacher-training materials

In any case, inservice training kits are needed. An introductory kit is usually needed for administrators who do not have the time to witness a teaching demonstration that is necessarily spread over two or three days. The kit usually includes a video that covers all levels of the programme.

Members of the project team need a separate teacher-training kit for each of the three stages of the programme. A kit usually includes such things as a video and a slide set, the teacher's manual, a few starter books, teacher's notes, and a set of overhead transparencies. In Thailand, the kit is used in conjunction with demonstration teaching, during four- or five-day teacher-training seminars.

Teacher-training kits assume importance only when dealing with large populations. In single-school situations, more can be done by demonstration and working with teachers than by talking and showing videos and slides.

The programme development schedule

In general, the literacy programme for each school grade is developed over a period of three years, in accordance with the following schedule.

First year
1. Outline of the programme for that grade level.
2. Development and trial of programme elements.

Second year
3. Writers' workshop for that grade.
4. Prototype version of the teacher's manual and training materials.
5. Piloting of the grade programme in schools.

Third year
6. Programme review.
7. Revision and printing of the starter books.
8. Revision and piloting of the teacher's manual.
9. Compilation of teacher's notes.
10. Revision and piloting of the training materials.

Fourth year
11. Printing of the starter books and teacher's manual.
12. Printing of the teacher's notes.
13. General implementation of the year's programme (in projects over 100 classrooms in size).

Conclusion

Whether it be a text, a teaching process, a video, a teacher's manual, or the entire programme for a year, every item goes through the four consecutive steps of developing, trialling, piloting, and implementing. The first three of these steps each take one year, and it is followed by revision of the item. For the developmental and pilot years only low-cost prototype versions of the programme materials are used. Finished versions are produced only in time for the general implementation phase in the fourth year.

The authors have learnt to adopt this unhurried approach to programme development for the very reason that they have been working in situations where there has been gross failure, so that fundamental changes have to be made in teacher and student behaviours. The fact that no published pupil materials are produced make possible further progressive development of the programme, even after the fourth year. If a programme unit or a starter book ought to be withdrawn because a better one may be devised, only the teacher's notes and/or the starter book for that one unit become obsolete. It should be reasonably easy, therefore, to prevent the programme from ossifying if the educational administrators remember that they have adopted CLE techniques for programme development, not a particular CLE programme.

Chapters 2 and 3 described the nature of CLE literacy teaching and of how teachers and students work together within CLE classroom activities; and Chapter 4 outlined a CLE programme for elementary schools, across several major dimensions. One further programme dimension – the assessment of learning and teaching – remains; and it is essential that assessment be based on the same understandings of language and learning if they are not to conflict with, and thereby mar, both the teaching and the programme building. In Chapters 5 and 6, Dr John Oller Jr deals with that remaining dimension of literacy teaching and programming.

CHAPTER 5

Testing literacy and related language skills: Part I, Review of theory

JOHN W. OLLER, Jr

Introduction

Tests are important because they define what the curriculum is about and what is expected of the curriculum, of the students, and of the teachers. In fact, tests probably define the objectives of schooling more exactly and with more binding power than any other sort of activity that takes place in a school context. The fact is that, just as a liquid seeks its own level, teaching will rise or fall to the level of the testing. If the expectations set by testing are high the teaching and learning will tend to rise to the challenge. If the level defined by the tests is mediocre or low, teaching will tend to sink to that level. Therefore, an approach to testing ought to be based on the best possible theory because it will tend to define curricular objectives in addition to most of what happens in the classroom. Part of the need for theory will be fulfilled by a clear idea of what the curriculum should consist of. Previous chapters of this book are about theory, curriculum, and its implementation in classroom activities. Now, in this chapter, we come to testing the sort of activity that can provide the practical milestones for the curriculum and its implementation. Teaching always tends toward the activities defined by tests. The tests define the ends in view throughout the educational process. These facts about the relation between theory, curriculum, teaching, and testing are shown in Fig. 5.1.

This chapter sums up and reviews theory in anticipation of the next, which gives examples of tests. The discussion of theory is consistent with that of previous chapters, although language is viewed from, perhaps, a slightly different perspective. It then presents five basic principles to be followed in testing (and in the curriculum at large). To exemplify the principles and show how they might work in hypothetical cases, a number of example tests that illustrate requirements laid down in the theory are

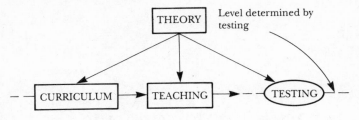

Figure 5.1: Curriculum and teaching will rise or fall to the level of the testing

discussed. Finally, the chapter concludes with some guidelines for teachers and educators to follow in implementing an integrated testing programme.

A review of theory

Language plays a central role in nearly any classroom. Language is even important to programmes aimed at athletics, dance, music, and art where movement, gesture, pictures, sculpture and action enjoy great importance as communicative devices. In fact, almost any educator will admit that literacy is at the heart of any well-rounded educational experience. Success in education depends largely on the degree to which children in schools are enabled to understand the connection between what the teacher says, what is written in the books, and what takes place in the world of experience. Success at school means understanding classroom discourse whether it is spoken or written, that is, it means understanding the curriculum, by linking it appropriately with the facts of experience. It might well be said that being educated is a matter of being able to negotiate many kinds of discourse relative to the world of experience.

In helping children to grow into mature, well-educated persons, schools are obliged to place a special emphasis on various forms of written discourse. Literacy means being able to understand and, in some cases, to produce, a fairly wide range of written materials. In the modern world of the 1990s, as we look towards the beginning of the third millennium AD, the techno-logical revolution has transformed itself into an increasingly abstract information processing revolution. In addition to being able to read, write, and handle numbers, literacy today increasingly means being able to find your way around a CRT (cathode ray tube), or a liquid-crystal screen, via a keyboard or 'mouse', and knowing the ins and outs of various kinds of computer software. Language plays a central role in all of this as well. However, our purpose is not merely to understand and appreciate the special role played by language in the modern world, but to get some notion about how to assess or measure those skills and abilities that being literate requires.

In testing literacy and the language skills that support and sustain it, two questions, as Richard Walker and Saowalak Rattanavich have stressed in earlier chapters, are critical: (1) What kinds of discourse must children learn to read, write, and use in other ways? And, (2) What range of uses must children become able to perform with the various kinds of discourse? The answers to these two questions, as pointed out in earlier chapters, will set the limits not only of the curriculum for literacy, but also of the tests that ought to be used in assessing its implementation.

From the curricular point of view, the teacher needs to know what kinds of things literate people are expected to be able to do and with what kinds of discourse. This will enable teachers to determine what kinds of situations to orchestrate in the classroom so that the children will learn to do those things with those kinds of discourse. For instance, in addition to being able to read and understand the writing seen on signs on doors, streets, and product labels, children need to be able to understand and talk about, as well as read and write, stories, descriptions, letters, resumés, summaries and the like. In addition to these standard forms of texts, as children grow and mature within and beyond their school experience, they should become able to handle many other kinds of texts such as news articles, editorials, advertisements, menus, price lists, catalogues, product guarantees, research reports, directions on medicine bottles, timetables (for buses, trains, and aeroplanes), invoices, sales agreements, contracts, maths problems, proofs, written instructions for assembling or using consumer goods, and so on. The question is how all of this growth and development can be brought about in school contexts.

Now, it is a fact that every literate person started out being non-literate and every language-user just as certainly began as an infant that could no more understand a particular language than any illiterate can read. So, how do infants become able to understand and speak a particular language and how do youngsters, who cannot read at first, become able to do so? The problem in both instances is summed up in Fig. 5.2.

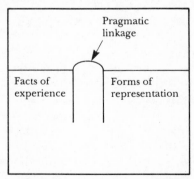

Figure 5.2: The process of making sense of discourse (pragmatic mapping)

The pre-linguistic infant becomes a language user by relating the conventional forms of a particular language (meaningful representations of a certain kind) to the facts of that infant's experience. By the same token, the pre-literate child who learns to read relates meaningful representations of a certain kind (visual representations of words or meanings in a particular language) to the facts of that child's experience. In both cases representations and facts are involved. In each instance, in order for the needed advance to be made, previously unknown and therefore incomprehensible representations must be related to more or less familiar facts. That is, the meanings of the representations (the special class of forms in a language or writing system, or both) must be determined relative to facts of experience.

The connections of the spoken or written forms to the relevant facts of experience must be unpacked. Names have to be linked to persons. Referring phrases must be linked to their objects that is, the things or abstract entities referred to. Predications must be associated with their particular meanings. Events must be identified and placed in their appropriate time frames. Whether an event, process, or state of being is perceived as ongoing or completed must be understood. Meanings intended by a particular person must be distinguished from ones not intended or possibly intended or understood by someone else. Meanings addressed to a particular consumer must be distinguished from those directed elsewhere. What is understood must be kept separate from what is meant. The problem of understanding discourse produced by someone else is to figure out what that person meant in constructing that discourse. What the producer means, however, in writing a text must be judged by that same producer according to what someone else is likely to understand from the text. In addition to all this, the person producing or interpreting discourse must assess it with respect to the facts of experience. It is necessary to make some sort of judgement about whether it is true of those facts (factual), merely resembles them (fictional), or is some sort of fantasy, play with words, irony, sarcasm, lie, joke, and so on.

What makes the unpacking problem solvable, difficult though it is, is that the facts to which representations at least purport to relate are already understood to some extent before we ever come to the problem of unpacking any particular discourse or other representation. The persons, objects, events, and relations of experience are already known in part through *sensory* impressions and in part through prior knowledge whether it is like the innate expectation that visible objects will be tangible or the sort of knowledge acquired from previous understandings of discourse. For example, in the case of the normal pre-lingual child it is the context of experience that helps the child to begin to understand utterances (and gestures) of others (or their writings) and eventually to begin to produce similar utterances (gestures, and writings). By the same token, the already established connection between utterances in a particular language and the facts of experience of, say, a normal post-lingual (talking) but pre-literate (not yet reading) child, will similarly help the pre-literate child to begin to become literate. The child first understands certain facts of experience through sensory impressions (sight, hearing, touch, smell, and taste) and later begins to connect these sensory representations with significant gestures and intonations patterns. Becoming able to return a smile, or to recognize a wave, or to react to pointing by looking in the right direction, to a certain intonation with an appropriate other intonation, would each qualify as growth in the gestural, paralinguistic, or *kinesic*, system. A little later still, the particular bodily gestures we call speech (the elements of the *linguistic* system) will come more and more to have special significance and begin to be unravelled in their special relations to facts. Even later still, written representations of speech gestures will come into view and begin to be unpacked by the child who is moving from pre-literacy into what Smith (1982) has called 'the literacy club'.

All of this is summed up in Fig. 5.3. The first kind of representation we learn to handle is sensory. We learn to recognize objects and events that we see, hear, touch, taste, and smell. Secondarily, we are aided very early in our development by significant movements, especially by the gestures of other persons around us. They point to particular objects and to ourselves. They show approval or disapproval in ways that mark objects and events as acceptable or unacceptable. They move or direct us through our environment. These significant gestures and movements of others have value mainly in guiding us in the way we manage and negotiate relations with things, events, and persons in our environment. At a third remove, and at a substantially higher level of abstraction, other persons use speech (assuming we can hear, or manual signs if we cannot). At a fourth remove from the facts, these significant linguistic forms may be spoken by someone else and only heard by us. Or at a fifth remove, they may eventually be spoken by us. At the sixth level of the diagram (and it must be noted that the levels are somewhat arbitrarily arranged and distinguished here) we come to the writings of others, and finally, at level seven, we come to writings that we ourselves produce. In Fig. 5.3, tape-recorded forms are not pictured, but all the representational forms that are shown serve to represent the facts of experience in abstract ways.

With linguistic forms aided by gestures and sensory information, for example, we can name or describe objects pointed to: 'See that small lizard, there, on the wall?' We can designate their attributes: 'He's so quick.' We can describe their actions: 'See how fast he moves?' We can call attention to characters: 'He has a long tail and stripes on his belly.' And so on. We can refer to facts through specifying subject–predicate relations: '[The lizard] $_{subject}$ [runs into the bushes] $_{predicate}$.' We can negate such

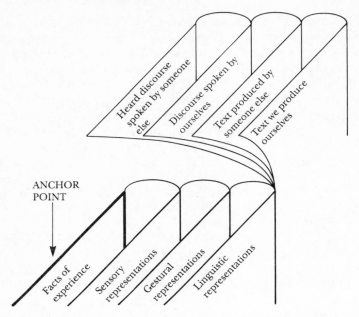

Figure 5.3: Expanding the pragmatic mapping of the facts of experience relative to representations of them (and vice versa – representations to facts)

relations: '[The lizard] subject [does [not] negation like to be approached by people] predicate.' We may also string such relations together through conjunction (e.g. by words like 'and') or we may subordinate one subject–predicate relation to another in a hierarchical way: '[[When] subordinator [the lizard [[that]subordinator is on the wall]subordinate clause sees me standing here] subordinate clause [he immediately runs away] main clause].' Referring to Fig. 5.3 again, facts are connected first to sensory experience, subsequently to gestures, and finally to language. In interpreting discourse in a linguistic form, therefore, the problem of comprehension is to determine the practical connections of the discourse forms with the facts of experience. Or, in producing discourse, the problem is to arrange forms in such a way that connections with facts which we choose to represent can be correctly determined by someone else.

What does such a theory teach us about a curriculum for literacy and about the kinds of classroom activities and tests that will help children to become literate? One lesson is that the interpreting of linguistic forms is aided by the construction of sensory and gestural representations. In keeping with all that Richard Walker and Saowalak Rattanavich have said in earlier chapters, this may be called the principle of *scaffolding*. It says that the richer the sensory and gestural information about the factual basis of any given discourse (whether spoken, signed, or written) the easier it will be for the consumer (learner, listener, reader) to determine the meanings of that discourse. Scaffolding, especially relevant when it comes to unfamiliar representations such as written ones are for anyone who is still pre-literate. In the early stages of becoming literate, supplementary context supplied through still or moving pictures, audio recordings, dramatization, games related to the textual meanings, manipulable illustrations, hands-on experimental activities, all will help the learner to be able to solve the closely related language and literacy problems, that is to link the unfamiliar forms with their respective meanings. Linguistic comprehension (whether in listening or reading activities) means unpacking the meanings intended by the producer(s) of the discourse as well as any additional meanings that are suggested by the facts of experience in relation to the forms of the discourse itself. All of this depends on correctly linking linguistic forms with facts of experience. For such a determination of meanings to be possible, there must *be* some determinate facts. Surprisingly, many educators (and theoreticians too, especially linguists), sad to say, are apt to omit this last and crucial step of connecting forms of representations with facts. They are apt to stress sounds, words, and discourse structures, or sound and letter correspondences (phonics), but forget about the facts of experience that those discourse elements represent. Without connection to such facts, discourse elements are empty. A nearly certain recipe for failure in any kind of language instruction is to try to get children to process linguistic forms that are essentially unrelated to any factual basis. The tendency is to err on the discourse side of the formula to emphasize surface forms of representations – sounds, letters, words, sentences, structures, functions of speech acts (the right-hand side of Fig. 5.2) at the expense of the factual side of the equation (the left-hand side of Fig. 5.2).

Teachers and curriculum writers are apt to assume that because they themselves have reached the stage where the abstract, universal, and virtual aspects of spoken and written discourse are accessible to them, this is an appropriate place for children (or other beginners) to start. Their assumption is false. Such educators have forgotten, because their learning took place mostly at a subconscious level, all the scaffolding they used in order to attain the abstract understanding they have of the meanings of words, written symbols, and so on. Therefore, they are inclined to throw away any scaffolding that would lead learners from facts in the real world to the highest forms of abstract reasoning. Instead these misguided educators, unaware of how they actually learnt and ever cognizant of how they have been taught to think people ought to learn, begin at some remote level. Often they dispense with the facts of experience and even the whole world itself in which those facts have meaning. Phonics approaches to reading, of course, are a classic case in point.

It is about as easy for a foreign language student to acquire an additional language, for a child to acquire the mechanics of written discourse, or for an illiterate to become literate by such methods as it would be to understand what is going on in a film where the utterances of the script are scrambled and the pictures, sound effects, and other supporting elements have been removed. The fact is that we really need to refer to particular facts of the world of experience and to the rich connections between such actual facts and the discourse that relates to those facts in order to solve difficult discourse processing problems such as acquiring a language or becoming literate. Even the acquisition of so-called 'mechanical' aspects of written discourse such as punctuation and spelling will benefit greatly from attention to tasks that take particular facts of the world of experience into consideration.

A handful of recommendations for testing (and teaching)

In keeping with the foregoing theory, here are five recommendations for the testing of language skills (and for teaching them) in relation to literacy programmes:

1. Always use a well-determined and preferably a well-motivated factual basis (i.e. use meaningful discourse or textual material that makes sense relative to a factual basis that is self-contained and is itself motivated, that is *don't use nonsense or pieces of text whose meanings cannot be determined*). For example, use a story, game, activity, dialogue, description, or any discourse that has a beginning and an end and that makes sense as a unit, i.e., that is determinately related to some known or demonstrable experiential basis. In ordinary experience sufficient motivation for discourse is usually supplied by a meaningful conflict or disequilibrium (one that interferes with the attainment of some desired goal), or in general a change that has surprise value relative to the execution of some on-going plan. Select motivated materials that are related in known ways to facts that are or can be made known to learners by some means other than the discourse forms per se. Remember that the learners need scaffolding to help them in unpacking the discourse elements. For instance, do not ever test (or try to teach) a single discourse element separated from the factual context that makes it meaningful. Do not test any isolated sound–symbol relation, vocabulary item, sentence out of the blue sky, or even a paragraph, an apology, a request, or a dialogue out of the blue. Do not (in the early stages) use a text that is abstract and difficult to illustrate with pictures, dramatization, and so on. If you want these kinds of linguistic devices to appear in your test, be sure to embed

them in a meaningful context where sufficient scaffolding is available to learners. *Never try to test bits and pieces of language without linking them to determinate facts of experience.* In other words, *never try to test single items of linguistic form in isolation from some particular, meaningful, demonstrable, factual context.*

2. Respect the facts (what's happening, who's involved, when, where, for what purposes, and so on) *don't ignore the real world.* Every teaching activity, question asked, or test item should relate to facts that are known or that can reasonably be inferred from ones that are known. *Never ask students to manipulate meaningless surface forms of language or text.* On the contrary, ask them about what happened, who was involved, when it happened, where, why George was in such a hurry, why the lizard runs when we approach it, and so on. If elements of surface form (particular sounds, words, structures, functions) need to be considered, they should be examined *in their respective factual contexts* but never in total isolation from such facts. For instance, if the name of a certain symptom relative to a medical prescription is in doubt, for example, say the word 'fever', for instance, then it might make sense to test that word, but only in relation to a fully developed and appropriate factual context. (A certain child in our story is sick. Mother feels his forehead and discovers he is burning up with fever. She takes his temperature, and so on.) These things can be pictured and dramatized. We can even harmlessly create the illusion of a fever by holding a hot wet cloth to our own or a child's forehead. Relative to such facts the term 'fever' can be given a determinate meaning and can be legitimately tested, but merely to say that 'temperature' is a synonym for 'fever' is of little use to anyone who does not yet know the connection of one or both of these terms with the facts of experience.

3. The performance assessed must involve the actual comprehension or expression of meaning relative to known facts: *we should never settle for surface-processing alone.* Never ask students merely to 'use a word in a sentence', or 'ask me a question using "if"', or 'find a word that rhymes with "time"', or 'ask me permission for three things you would like to do', 'give five different ways to apologize for missing an appointment', 'explain how you would ask someone to stop bothering you at the airport', and so on. Of course, it may be important to find out if a language user knows the meaning of a particular word, or even how that word sounds if it is uttered. It may be necessary to find out if a user understands a particular syntactic structure, or whether to take a particular statement as a request, order, suggestion, and so on. However, meanings, sounds, syntactic categories, morphological devices, connective relations, indirect speech acts, and the like, are important precisely because they may be used to determine different facts. There-

fore, nothing whatever will be lost of the sounds, words, phrases, structures, functions, and so on, if we refer always to determinate facts in a well-developed meaningful context. On the contrary, much will be gained.

4. Aim for processing under normal time constraints: *do not teach or test indefinitely shrunken down or expanded half-second segments of reading.* Very rapid tachistoscopic presentations of words may be interesting to certain experimental psychologists, but they generally make a poor basis for a reading curriculum or almost any sort of reading test. Also, at the other end of the time-scale, avoid using activities or tests that allow unrealistically large amounts of time to complete a task. For instance, allowing examinees sufficient time in reading a text to look up every word in a bilingual dictionary would rarely qualify as normal language processing. Nor is writing single words from dictation (as in a traditional spelling test), with long pauses between items, a normal listening task. Normal language processing usually involves a rate of discourse presentation that is at least equal to (or sometimes faster than) a normal rate of speech. A better way of testing spelling, and a great deal of discourse processing capability as well, would be to give a dictation at a normal rate of speech with pauses between natural phrase or clause boundaries. (See below for more about how to give dictation.) Reading silently can proceed, normally, even more rapidly than speech. Writing takes more time, but even here there are limits. A friendly letter that takes more than a year of concentrated energy to write will probably never get written. While in teaching there may be cases where allowing large amounts of time is desirable, in testing this should generally be avoided. Language processing should be expected to occur at a reasonable, normal, rate.

5. The questions or discourse-processing performances asked of the students in a test (or in a teaching activity) should aim at the central elements of the text or discourse the kinds of things that intelligent, normal people would be expected to notice or talk about. For instance, in a narrative where there is a dog-fight and one of the dogs ends up dead on the pavement, it would be odd to ask whether or not there was a yellow cat lurking in the shadows nearby, or how many taxis passed while the dog-fight was in progress, if a fly buzzed past Sam's ear, if one of the on-lookers spoke Chinese, how much time elapsed between the honking of a car horn and the miaowing of the cat while the battle raged, and so on. On the other hand, details that have some bearing on the story (that the German shepherd's thick collar helped him to overcome the fierce Doberman) or actions that might be understood as relevant to the facts depicted (e.g. the need for dog owners to keep their animals off the street) are fair game for test questions.

Exemplifying tests

This section defines testing, discusses its foundational grounding in the facts of experience, sets the limits of what can be legitimately tested, and offers some examples of ways to approach testing, especially in the classroom. It is important to bear in mind that the example tests to be given here are merely for the sake of illustration. The examples themselves are not intended as particular tests to be applied in any actual classroom setting. Rather, they are intended to illustrate *kinds of tests* as well as *kinds of testing activities* that can be *developed from and applied to any factual discourse basis that meets the requirements laid down in our theory*. The purpose here is to illustrate applications of the theory and the five caveats (derived from that theory) which were just stated in the previous section.

The starting point for test construction (on any curricular activity, for that matter), according to our theory, is to select a suitable, factual, discourse basis. In previous chapters these have been referred to as 'concentrated language encounters'. Such a factual basis might come directly from the experience of a single child in the classroom, or it might be supplied by the teacher (or taken from a book or videotape or other source). It might involve an event or series of events that the child shares with other children in the classroom. For instance, in a certain classroom context a first-grader told about a burglar breaking into her house over the weekend, by climbing through a window, right across her sleeping baby brother's crib, and taking out the TV and stereo through the front door. The little girl was concerned for her baby brother's safety, but fortunately he was unharmed. Such a story, recounted by the child could form the (factual) basis for a 'big book' and a great many spin-off activities including a host of tests drawing upon that factual context.

Alternatively, the discourse basis might be a story, game, activity, experiment, field-trip, or some other element of the curriculum. The story could be one provided by the teacher, or taken from a book. The important thing in choosing a discourse basis for teaching and testing is that any given choice should be one of a suitable difficulty level, not too easy or too difficult, and that it be interesting, based on facts that are easy to illustrate, dramatize, and thus, to communicate about and learn from. Further, the factual basis is what will largely determine the validity of our testing activities. Selecting a suitable discourse basis for testing (and, of course, for teaching) may be more a matter of art than science, but there is no way around the choice. The test writer (or teacher) must face up to the task of selecting from the myriad activities, materials, and incidentals that go to make up the curriculum, the sort of factual basis that will provide a grounding for testing activities. Here some intelligent, sensitive, subjective judgement is called for. The decisions required are essentially the same as those that go into the making of a big book, or the selection of a site for a field-trip, or the choice of a game, experiment, or activity to use or foster in the classroom or on the playground.

In addition to considering factors such as interest, dramatizability, level of difficulty, motivation, and the like, the test writer also needs to take into consideration the purpose of the testing. According to the theory advocated in this book there ought not be any testing whatever that does not contribute in a positive way to the clarification (the very definition) of what the curriculum and the whole school experience is about. Only tests and testing activities that help learners and teachers alike to define their objectives should be used. In other words, the tests ought always to be integral parts of the curriculum. They ought to be good teaching tools. Further, if the caveats listed in the immediately preceding section are taken seriously, since the tests are to be based on discourse forms that have been systematically linked to actual facts in the experience of the children to be tested, the test itself *is a teaching device*. It helps learners to understand both the discourse and its relation to the known facts. For this reason, it will do no harm for teachers to use tests as tests per se and at the same time to use them as teaching tools.

CHAPTER 6

Testing literacy and related language skills: Part II, Examples of testing procedures and activities

JOHN W. OLLER, Jr

Introduction

Before giving examples of actual testing activities that might be developed it will be useful to define the term 'test'. What is to count as a test? In fact, any discourse processing performance that can be judged as better or worse relative to some normative standard can be qualified as a test. All that is required is that the rater (the tester, teacher, or whatever rater or group of raters are involved) have a reliable notion of what a better or worse performance on the task in question consists of. A task that meets this minimal testing requirement may be called a *scalable* test. That is to say, performances can be rated on a scale ranging from better to worse. Most language processing tasks, where the factual basis (as discussed in the preceding chapter) is known, will qualify as tests in this minimal sense. Examples would include such things as telling a story, summarizing an argument, recounting a conversation, explaining a process, describing a scene, giving a speech, taking part in a drama, and so on.

A more stringent requirement for a test is that it be *scorable*, in other words, it must be possible to reduce a performance of the task to a number that represents right or wrong answers, or some determinable quantity. Not all scalable tasks tasks meet this more stringent requirement, though all scorable tasks must, in principle, always be scalable. Of the class of scorable tasks, a still smaller set of so-called 'objective' tests exist which can be reduced to marks on an answer sheet or other device (e.g. a keyboard or computer screen) that can be mechanically scored. Further, there probably are tasks which are so indeterminate (usually because no factual basis for them can be determined) as to be unscalable. In general, when the facts to which a given discourse performance relates are unknown or cannot be determined, the performance itself will not be reliably scalable or scorable. It will not serve as an adequate basis for a test.

The kinds of tasks that might qualify as tests can be summed up in Fig. 6.1. Discourse tasks can be divided, loosely, into

1. indeterminate ones (which are unsuitable as tests or as teaching activities);
2. those that are determinate and therefore at least scalable (which minimally qualify as potential tests or as teaching activities);
3. those that are sufficiently determinate to be both scalable and scorable (i.e. ones that are especially useful for classroom purposes);
4. those that are machine-scorable (those most commonly used in wide-scale institutional testing).

Generally, at the national, provincial, district, or even school-wide levels, only machine scorable tests will be applied, while individual classroom teachers will generally prefer tests that fall into categories (2) and (3), that is that are determinate enough at least to be scalable and in many cases also scorable.

Admittedly, for some institutional purposes, it will occasionally be necessary to use screening procedures that are not machine-scorable. Some test specialists see this as a disadvantage owing to the fact that a 'subjective' element of judgement enters the rating of any non-mechanical scoring procedure. However, what such specialists overlook is that the same sort of 'subjective' judgement enters any scoring or rating whatever including the kind that ultimately depends on an optical scanner or other mechanical device. The fact is that someone (or some group) must decide in advance of any machine scoring what the correct answers are to the test items. At the point where those decisions are made, a machine-scorable test is no more 'objective' than any merely scalable task is.

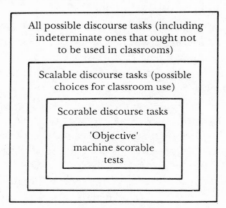

All possible discourse tasks (including indeterminate ones that ought not to be used in classrooms)

Scalable discourse tasks (possible choices for classroom use)

Scorable discourse tasks

'Objective' machine scorable tests

Figure 6.1: Kinds of discourse tasks viewed and classified as kinds of tests

In fact, there is no guarantee whatever that a machine-scorable test will even be more *reliable* (much less that it will be more *valid*) than any test which is not machine scorable. Of course, *reliability* is defined merely as the degree to which a test tends to produce the same results under the same conditions on different occasions, while *validity* is a more stringent requirement. The degree of validity is the extent to which the test actually measures whatever it purports to measure. Now, as to *scorer reliability*, it is true that a machine will usually make fewer errors in scoring than a human scorer might make, but even this is not guaranteed. For instance, certain items in the key used by the machine can be marked incorrectly and result in inaccuracies throughout all the test scores. Or, a given test-taker or any number of them may correctly mark the answer sheets but in ways that the machine does not recognize, for example by using too light a pencil, or making an 'X' through wrong answers, or by using ink instead of graphite, or by getting off by one number and giving all the right answers but to questions numbered 2 through 101 instead of 1 through 100, by crossing out wrongly marked answers instead of erasing them completely, by not filling in the machine-scored bubbles completely, and so on. Human scorers would be apt to spot some of these sources of unreliability and, in such cases, could generate more accurate scores than any current mechanical optical-scanner would be apt to. At any rate, it is inaccurate to suppose that all the subjectivity (i.e. human judgement) has been removed from any machine-scorable 'objective' test.

With the foregoing definitions in mind, we are ready to consider what can be tested in a fact-based discourse. A little later we will go on to consider some examples of actual testing activities that might be applied to a wide range of discourse types. The objective cannot be to illustrate all possible techniques, as that would be impossible, but we can set certain definite limits to the kinds of fact-based items that can be included in the kinds of tests that are recommended. Suppose we use the following narrative about the burglary the first-grader reported. This narrative, or one not very different from it, might form the basis for a big book and the various activities related to its construction, illustration, and mastery by a group of children who are in the process of becoming literate.

The Burglary

Hi. My name is Suzie. On Saturday night, a burglar broke into our apartment. He came through a window. He stepped right across my baby brother's crib. My brother was asleep. He didn't wake up. Everyone else was asleep too. I was asleep. My grandmother was asleep. My mother was asleep. The burglar took the TV and stereo and went right out the front door. Nobody saw him, but we figured out what happened the next morning.

Supposing the children in the classroom (or whatever children are to be tested) already know the language in which the narrative is told, this text may not be too difficult even for fairly early beginners.

Fortunately, even if they do not know the language, much can be done to simplify its presentation and thus to enable the children to acquire the language while they are developing an understanding of the facts of the story. For instance, the events can be acted out. The facts can be portrayed, partially at least, through pictures and illustrations. One of the great advantages of narratives, or in fact of any coherent text (as contrasted with nonsense or less coherent material), is that it is potentially infinitely rich in logical connectedness. A coherent discourse can always be simplified through summarization or it can be expanded. The expansion can be developed either by reading between the lines or by inferring what probably came before or what followed after the facts expressed in the narrative. For instance, the text might be condensed into a single sentence: 'A thief broke into Suzie's house on Saturday night.' Or, it might be expanded. For instance, we may assume that the thief had the intention to steal before he broke into the house and that after doing so he intended to sell the stolen goods. Maybe he did so to support a drug habit. Probably, he did not harm the sleeping infant because his purpose was to steal something of value that he could sell in order to get money. Harming the infant would not have served the thief's purpose – and so forth.

The same sorts of logical manipulations are possible with any coherent text. They are possible because textual structure is such that it sustains certain kinds of inference. It can be proved rigorously that all kinds of discourse comprehension (and production as well) are based on inference. From this it follows that all tests or test items (as well as curricular materials) must ultimately depend on inference. Further, we have seen in the previous chapter why it is that *only* fact-based discourse processing activities ought to be used in assessing (or teaching) literacy and language skills. Any approach to testing (or teaching) which depends on discourse forms separated from their connection to a factual basis is an approach that lacks the necessary basis for determining the meanings of those discourse forms. The scaffolding that is essential to learners in order for them to reach the highest levels of abstraction and generalization (the heights of inferencing) will be absent. Therefore, only fact-based discourse (not excluding plausible fictions that can be illustrated or dramatized with actual facts) should be used in any teaching or testing activity.

It remains to illustrate a sufficiently wide range of fact-based testing activities to adequately cover the broad scope of discourse genres and uses of them that a thorough-going curriculum ought to include. In order to illustrate the kinds of test activities that might be used in, say, a first-grade classroom (or other school context) we will refer to the narrative about the burglary as told by Suzie on p. 69. Let us suppose that the curriculum is organized (as recommended throughout this book) so that the facts of the discourse (absolutely any discourse) introduced into the classroom are first made known to students through drama, realia, pictures, illustrations, and other methods that are more or less directly accessible to the senses.

Suppose, for instance, that the narrative about the burglary is told and acted out by Suzie, or is dramatized with the help of the teacher and class members, for example one who plays the sleeping infant, another who plays the burglar, and so on. Or alternatively, imagine that a very similar story is actually presented in a cartoon form on videotape. The facts of the narrative, in either of these cases, can be known abductively to such an extent that the knowledge of the facts becomes a substantial foundation together with the sort of inferential scaffolding described above upon which to build a rich and deep comprehension of the spoken discourse, written forms of it, and all of the associated language and literacy skills that may be required. For instance, after the facts have been established through drama or film, names, phrases, and whole sentences can be attached to the dramatized or pictured events. At first, this ought to be done with spoken forms and soon after with written ones. For instance, the child (or cartoon character) who plays the part of the burglar can wear an appropriate label printed on a card, 'The burglar', as can all of the other objects and characters of the story. Even the events can be labelled with captions in a cartoon style book. As comprehension deepens as a result of multiple passes through the story, and as the language forms are enriched at each phase of development and on each successive pass through the story, more written elements may be introduced. Eventually all of it is put down in a 'big book' that is illustrated by drawings done by the children themselves.

Yes/No questions

Testing activities are worked into the curriculum all along the way. For instance, the first testing the teacher needs to do is to determine if the children have understood the facts. To begin with, a series of 'yes/no' questions are appropriate. These are pragmatically the simplest sorts of questions and if they focus on facts that can be known abductively from happenings that the children have actually experienced through the drama or cartoon film, the answers to such questions can be largely determined by the most basic sort of ground-level abductive reasoning. For instance, here is a series of 'yes/no' questions that covers the basic facts in the burglar narrative. Questions such as these would be appropriate in a first-grade class where the children are not yet really comfortable in the language of the classroom (e.g. in a classroom where the teacher speaks Thai, say, and the children speak Mandarin, or some other language):

Yes/No questions for 'The Burglar' narrative

[Teacher points to Suzie or a picture of Suzie and asks] 'Is this Suzie?'
[Teacher points to a picture of the burglar and asks] 'Is this Suzie's brother?'
[Pointing to the baby's crib] 'Is this grandmother's bed?'

The questions asked ought to cover the full range of facts in the story starting with the most obvious, central facts, and working up to details that are less easily understood. The questions suggested as examples would actually be quite difficult for children who are trying to become literate in a language they do not yet know. The list of such questions that are possible on the basis of any coherent fact-based discourse can be expanded indefinitely. A good rule would be to begin with questions requiring only the most obvious abductive inferences and then to move through the story without expecting the children to express any inductions or any abstract deductive inferences at all. Although noting that a burglar is a thief is a simple thing for someone who speaks English, for a child who is in the process of acquiring a language, that sort of inference (which depends on abstract syntactic and semantic relations between words) may be beyond reach. A lot of scaffolding will be required in order for the child to be able to get up to such a rarefied atmosphere of abstraction. Even the inductive generalization that the burglar is apt to sell the TV and stereo is way beyond the sort of thing a beginning language learner could be expected to say or even to understand. Of course, such an inductive inference, or other inferences of a deductive sort, would be possible from the very start for children who already know the language of instruction.

'Wh-' questions

At a slightly higher remove, after the second or third pass through the story (e.g. two or three screenings of the film), or even sooner if the children already know the language in question, 'wh-' questions may be introduced. At first, the questions should be answerable in single words. Later, whole phrases may be required. Later still, entire sentences may be within reach. Again, the earliest questions, especially with children who are working in a second language situation, ought to focus on the sorts of facts that are central to the story and also obviously portrayed in pictures or dramatization. Here are a few 'wh-' questions.

'Wh-' questions for 'The Burglar' narrative

[Teacher points to a picture of Suzie] 'Who is this?' *Suzie.*
[Pointing to a picture of the burglar] 'Who is this?' *(the) burglar.*
[Pointing to the window over the baby's crib] 'What is this?' *(the) window.*

'How did the burglar get in?' *Through the window.*
'Who was in the crib?' *Suzie's baby brother.*

So far, the answers to all of the questions asked have been contained in the facts and actual statements in the text. Nevertheless, it is relatively easy in constructing such questions to generate a list in each case that involves a progression from the simplest and most obvious facts to more complex and/or less obvious ones. However, in getting children to really master a text a great deal more work is possible within the limits of the statements actually made in the narrative version of the story.

Elicited imitation

For instance, children might be expected to be able to repeat the story, line by line. This sounds extremely simple (perhaps even too simple) but it will present some special challenges to children who are not native speakers of the language in question, or who may not have progressed even in their first language acquisition as far as the teacher may believe them to have progressed. Even for children who already know the language of the narrative, this task will probably not be performed quite flawlessly by all of the children. Research shows that children adjust discourse forms to fit the level of their own developing grammar. As a result, repetitions are often far from exact.

An elicited imitation task for 'The Burglar' narrative

[Teacher says] 'Hi. My name is Suzie.' [Students repeat] *Hi. My name is Suzie.*
'On Saturday night, a burglar broke into our apartment.' *On Saturday night, a burglar broke into our apartment.*

Obviously, the preceding question tasks (yes/no and 'wh-' types) are scorable. We may simply count the number of correct responses to each question. If those tasks were used as teaching activities, and if the children understood the narrative as well as we would expect them to, the scores should all be nearly perfect. That is, in each such task we should expect mastery of the material up to that level. However, when it comes to the elicited imitation task (a sentence repetition task), scoring is not so obvious and straightforward. If the task is tape-recorded it can be meticulously scored for every phoneme (or distinctive sound segment), syllable, morpheme (distinctive unit of meaning or grammatical function), word, phrase, or sentence used in the elicitation task. Even suprasegmental elements such as intonations and stress patterns may be examined for conformity to those used in the text.

The question usually asked concerning each unit of a given type, words being the most commonly scored element, is whether the unit in question is a recognizable reproduction of the one that was supposed to be produced at that juncture in the sequence of elements. If extraneous elements are inserted, or if necessary elements are left out, the score is accordingly reduced by the number of omitted or added elements. Otherwise the total score on the whole task is the number of elements of a given type (e.g. words) that are correctly produced and in the right order. The total possible score is the number of elements of the type scored appearing in the sentences or other sequences presented for repetition. Since words are, in most languages, the most obvious bundles of meanings, they are generally selected as the units to be scored. For instance, in the first sentence in the example given above, there are five words. In the next there are nine. In all, if the whole narrative were used in the form given above (p. 69), the total possible word score would be seventy-seven (treating as separate words items written between spaces or separated by a hyphen). If phonemes were used as the scored units the total possible score would be much higher. The total number of syllables would be about a third the number of phonemes. The number of phrases would be fewer than the words. And the number of sentences only eleven (counting the first string, 'Hi. My name is Suzie.' as only one sentence).

Moreover, since words and higher structures are made up of phonemes and syllables, and since words constitute the phrases and sentences, scoring for almost any single unit amounts to a partial accounting for the other units. Because words are the units of language that users are probably most conscious of as they speak, perhaps they are the best choice for scoring. However, there is no argument against scoring for other units as well. If sentences are chosen as the unit for scoring, a scale where 3 represents a perfect reproduction, 2, a recognizable but imperfect reproduction, 1, a reproduction that contains at least some recognizable element, and 0, a completely unrecognizable attempt or mere silence, will work very well and can, with just a little practice, be applied without the necessity of tape-recording the responses of each examinee. Or, an even rougher scale may be used if the teacher is using the task as a teaching device in which case the only distinction may be between perfect and nearly perfect reproductions of the elicited material. For teaching purposes, where mastery or nearly perfect performance is the goal, in the early stages it may be useful to cut the discourse up into smaller segments and then later join them into larger sequences. For example, 'Hi. My name is Suzie,' might be broken up into three items: (1) 'Hi.' (2) 'My name' (3) 'is Suzie.' If this is done, whether or not for teaching purposes, the breaks in discourse segments should be inserted only at phrasal boundaries and the stress and intonation patterns on the segmented items should be retained. They should not be presented as items in a list, but rather as segments of the larger discourse with which students are already familiar.

Some educators react negatively to elicited imitation on account of it being 'a purely rote task based only on short-term memory', or so they argue. It is easy to prove that this objection does not hold. If the discourse material has been presented in the manner prescribed in this chapter, and throughout this book, the discourse meanings have already achieved representation at deeper levels of processing that is, beyond short-term memory. The learner knows what the facts are. These are represented in long-term memory and in forms such as visual images and sequences of them, accompanying gestures, and abstract inferences, and so on.

All these are distinct from the surface elements of the original narrative. Those surface elements have become associated with actions, persons, events, and so on. Therefore, any element of surface form (a phoneme, syllable, word, phrase, or sentence) that is presented in the sort of elicited imitation task recommended here will have already been linked to abstract conceptualizations (semantic and syntactic categories) and to concrete meanings (facts) that are far removed from the surface-forms of the discourse and that cannot possibly be accessed at all without doing some of the kinds of pragmatic mapping described above in Figs 5.1, 5.2, and 5.3.

Now, the sort of 'rote memorization' that can be based exclusively on surface forms, say, sounds and syllables (held in short-term memory) cannot involve the deeper pragmatic connections our procedure guarantees. If it did involve them, the objection to 'rote memory' would evaporate instantly. In fact, any sequence of elements that exceeds short-term memory, if it is understood, assures us that the representational form in question has been linked to other representational forms that were not presented recently enough to have been provided to short-term memory. Imagine trying to repeat a sequence of words in a language you do not know that says something as complex as any five-to-fifteen-word segment of 'The Burglary' text. Even if some individual segment, or even all the segments of the discourse, could be managed by rote, the whole discourse could hardly be understood without going far beyond mere storage and recall of surface elements from short-term memory.

Furthermore, in the sort of application of elicited imitation recommended here, the teacher has already assured deeper levels of processing by preceding any elicited imitation task with the sorts of dramatization of the facts, followed by the question-asking procedures described earlier. In addition, the kinds of tasks (including scorable tests) to be introduced subsequently (in this chapter) will virtually remove all possibility of the discourse being understood only at the level of surface elements. Short-term memory will invariably be (as it always necessarily is) an important part of the processing of the elicited segments of the discourse, but it will certainly not be the only basis. It will not even be an adequate basis, by itself, to support comprehension of the dramatization of the discourse, or the cartoon-style film. Nor will it sustain correct answers to the question tasks described earlier, much less the more complex tasks yet to follow (see below).

Reading aloud

As soon as the children have understood the discourse well enough to reproduce it in a spoken form, they are ready to go on to more complex processing activities. Whether these tasks are to be regarded as teaching exercises or as tests is mainly a matter of preference and whatever immediate purpose the task best serves. Assuming the purpose includes instilling literacy skills in children who have not yet acquired those skills, we need to go on to tasks that introduce or expand upon previously introduced written versions of the discourse we are working with. Suppose that a 'big book' has been constructed containing the very sentences given above (p. 69). A variant of the elicited imitation task would be one where the segments are presented in a written form and the problem for the student is to read the segment aloud. By adding the written form into the curriculum at this point we invite the child to make the connections not only between the written form and the spoken version (the latter of which we have already shown that the child knows through the elicited imitation task), but we rely, as always, on all of the deeper levels of scaffolding already established through other pragmatic mapping activities. The facts are known. The sequence of events, persons involved, setting, and outcome are all established. The spoken forms of the utterances have been correctly linked up with the facts, and the child can produce those spoken forms in segment lengths that exceed the limits of short-term memory.

As a result we have (deliberately, with the child's interest at heart) reduced the difficulty of the task of reading the printed elements to a manageable level even for a child who is just barely beginning to move towards membership in the literacy club. The task can be made just a little easier by the teacher (tester) providing prompts, for example a partial or full spoken variant of the written forms just before asking the child to read the given segment aloud. Or, supposing we need to make the task more challenging, the prompts can be omitted and the segments to be read aloud can be lengthened until the children are actually fluently reading aloud the entire big book. In a test situation, the segments to be read aloud can be presented on large cards, one segment at a time, or on an overhead projector, or with a slide projector. Making up the cards, transparencies, or slides could also easily be converted into a teaching activity in which the children participate. The scoring of such tasks can be done in essentially the same ways that elicited imitation tasks are scored.

Copying written discourse

As soon as the children are reading the big book, or even some portion of it, they are in a position to begin writing it as well. There is no reason to postpone writing until the second grade. On the contrary, there are many reasons that reading and writing tasks need to be closely linked with each other and with listening and speaking tasks. If we want the children to succeed at the tasks we set (and on our tests), it should always be our goal (but especially in the early phases) to provide as much scaffolding as we can to enable that success. Listening to another child or to the teacher producing a spoken version of a certain discourse about facts that the child readily understands from a drama or other illustration, provides an additional level of representation that is linked to the facts. As soon as that heard form of representation has been understood (to whatever degree it is understood), this understanding becomes a level of scaffolding which will help in the comprehension and production of the corresponding spoken form (see Fig. 5.3). Similarly, the elicited spoken form, once it is mastered, constitutes a level of scaffolding from which yet other forms can be reached and subsequently mastered.

In the initial phases of writing, segments of the big book can be presented for short durations, as in the manner of presenting segments on cards, transparencies, or slides, for reading aloud. Only here, at an early phase of writing, the task set the examinee (learner) is to read the presented segment and then write it down. In the earliest phase of this sort of writing activity, the problem of forming the letters will be sufficiently challenging that even single words from the big book will exceed the limits of the child's capacity to hold the material in short-term memory. However, as the child becomes more familiar with the shapes of letters and with larger written segments of the discourse, it will be useful to present sequences of words or even whole sentences. At first it may be necessary for children to refer to the written version of a given word repeatedly in order to create a recognizable written variant of it. As the written forms become still more familiar, longer segments can be presented and for even shorter durations. These productions, as in the case of spoken-forms produced by elicited imitation or reading aloud, can be scored in similar ways. An added element will be the legibility of the written forms. Legibility in writing parallels pronunciation (clear and distinct articulation) in speaking. Elements present in the scoring of written productions that are not present in spoken-forms would include the so-called mechanics of spelling, capitalization, and punctuation.

Provided our testing (and teaching) never relates to anything other than fact-based, whole discourse, the full richness of the mechanics of written forms will be assured. In addition, the entire complex of the known facts and the previously mastered spoken and written forms will help the child in solving the special problems associated with the mechanics of writing. In such a rich context of fact-based discourse, supported by multiple levels of scaffolding from dramatization and illustration of meanings, the child will be at an optimal advantage to understand the abstract meanings of such mechanical aspects of writing as spelling, capitalization, and punctuation. But, remove such scaffolding and these aspects of written discourse will continue to baffle the children about as much as they do many present-day curriculum specialists.

Taking dictation

So far, the children have observed and understood the facts of the discourse from its dramatization. They have heard and understood its spoken form. They have listened to and reproduced the spoken form sentence-by-sentence. They have seen the written forms associated with the familiar discourse. They have heard these forms associated with spoken versions of the discourse. They have read the written forms aloud and they have learnt to write those written forms. They are now ready, owing to the scaffolding now in place, to write from dictation. A spoken version of the text may be presented segment-by-segment for children to write down. They have already linked the teacher's speech forms to speech forms they themselves produce. They have linked those same speech forms to written ones the teacher produced. They linked those written forms the teacher produced back to the speech forms of the teacher. Subsequently they linked the written forms produced by the teacher to spoken forms the children themselves produced (reading aloud). Later, they linked the written forms produced by the teacher to written forms they themselves produced. Dictation as a testing (or teaching) task simply takes the last representational form (a written version produced by the student) and links it back to the teacher's spoken version of the familiar discourse.

As in the case of all the other elicitation devices designed to assess (or to instil) familiarity with one or another form of the fact-based discourse, dictation too is an elicitation device. The teacher (or someone else, either live or on a tape-recording of some sort) presents a segment of the discourse in a spoken version and the task set the children is to write down the segment that they have just heard. As in all such tasks, the difficulty may be adjusted upward or downward by giving longer or shorter segments of text respectively, or by slowing down the rate of speech, repeating the segment one or more times, providing prompts, and so on. In a test situation, though we want children to succeed, we also want to challenge them to ever higher levels of achievement and to assure that the kind of processing we ask them to do in the test situation really moves them towards the kind of processing the whole curriculum aims to enable them to perform. Therefore, we would ordinarily not dictate single words. We would want to use segments of, say, five or more words, so as to challenge short-term memory.

In the version of 'The Burglary' discourse that follows, each slash inserted in the text, marks a segment boundary, or pause point. At each of these indicated junctures, the person giving the dictation must allow sufficient time for the children to write down what they have just heard. The amount of time needed here will vary with the level of literacy of the children being tested. A simple way of creating a pause that corresponds to the length and complexity of the segment just uttered is for the person giving the dictation to repeat the segment sub-vocally and to spell it out (silently) one, two, or more times.

The Burglary

Hi. My name is Suzie./On Saturday night,/a burglar broke into our apartment./He came through a window./He stepped right across/my baby brother's crib./My brother was asleep./He didn't wake up./Everyone else was asleep too./I was asleep./My grandmother was asleep./My mother was asleep./The burglar took the TV and stereo/and went right out the front door./Nobody saw him,/but we figured out what happened the next morning./

The objective is to present a segment that is comprehensible, bounded by natural syntactic and/or other junctures, and challenging enough that the child must comprehend the meaning of that segment by working-up a representation of the facts referred to by it. We want dictated segments to be associated with the facts of the discourse as well as with its surface forms both spoken and written. We do not want it to be possible for the child to link the surface form of speech directly with the surface forms of writing without understanding the meaning of either one. In general, this is not possible if we work with significant segments of a whole, fact-based discourse. A direct, short-circuited association between spoken and written surface forms can only occur in something like a traditional spelling test where some of the meanings of at least some of the words are not known to the child but the surface forms (both spoken and written) are known. Such a short circuit cannot obtain if we are using significant multi-syllabic words and phrases of a whole, fact-based discourse. There are many assurances from other tests (teaching activities) that the children really do know the meanings of the surface forms in question. Furthermore, by presenting long enough segments of speech between pauses, we can be certain that short-circuit surface linkages are impossible even for any single segment. If the segment is too long to manage in short-term memory without deep level comprehension a direct association between mere surface-forms cannot be effected by the child. The meaning of both the spoken and written forms must be understood in order to associate them with each other.

Scoring of dictation can proceed exactly as the scoring of the other elicitation procedures described above, so no more needs to be said on that account. Instead, it is time to move on to consider kinds of processing tasks that will ensure still deeper levels of processing. So far, the question-based tests as well as the elicitation devices discussed (imitation, reading aloud, copying, and dictation) all depend fairly exclusively either on specific facts already referred to in the discourse and their connection to particular surface forms (which have also already been provided) or they depend on connections between different surface-forms (e.g. spoken versus written ones) which are deeply interrelated with each other at the level of the facts (see Fig. 5.3 and its explanation). It is time now in our testing (or teaching) activities to go on to consider tasks that more directly demand inferences of an inductive sort, or the production of forms not directly provided in any prior discourse sustained by short-term memory. It is time to move on also to deductively based semantic and syntactic relations as well as inferences that reach inductively beyond what is stated in the discourse.

Cloze exercises

An open-ended cloze exercise is the sort of test (or teaching device) that omits words from a discourse, usually a written text, and requires examinees to guess the missing words. Even if the discourse is a familiar one, such guesses are generally sustained by deductive and inductive inferences that reach beyond the particular facts that can be abductively inferred from the discourse. Such cloze exercises can be done orally or in written form. Here is an example of such an exercise where every fifth word has been deleted from 'The Burglary' discourse.

> (I)   Hi. My name is (1) ——. On Saturday night, a (2) —— broke into our apartment. (3) —— came through a window. (4) —— stepped right across my (5) —— brother's crib. My brother (6) —— asleep. He didn't wake (7) ——. Everyone else was asleep (8) ——. I was asleep. My (9) —— was asleep. My mother (10) —— asleep. The burglar took (11) —— TV and stereo and (12) —— right out the front (13) ——. Nobody saw him, but (14) —— figured out what happened (15) —— next morning.

An oral version of this exercise could be given where the teacher would read the narrative in as normal an intonation as possible but pausing at each blank. The task set the listeners would be to supply the missing words. Supposing the written version of the text was not before them at the time, examinees would have to base their guesses on their prior acquaintance with the specific facts of the story (abductive inferences), plus expectations based on previously supplied information (inductive inference), as well as whatever semantic and syntactic information the text provides concerning the requirements of surface forms (deductive inferences), and or, of course, combinations of these. In an oral cloze task, usually the teacher confirms or supplies the correct answers as she goes along, while in a written task, examinees only have the written context plus their previous guesses to help them figure out what goes in any subsequent blank.

Consider the cloze exercise given above. Assuming the examinees know the facts of the story, they should be able to guess 'Suzie' for item (1). The main support for this inferential choice is the fact known abductively (from previous experience) that the story is told by Suzie. This choice also gains some deductive support from the fact that the story-teller is a little girl and 'Suzie' is typically a name for a girl and the diminutive '-ie', an affectionate designation for a small child. However, as soon as the correct answer is known abductively, such deductive additions (from the semantics of the name) support it redundantly.

The solution to item (2) is aided by the deduction that someone who breaks and enters is some sort of criminal, but this deduction, though necessarily correct as far as it goes, is not specific enough to determine that the criminal in question was a burglar and not some other sort of criminal. Prior memory of the facts provide a complete solution to the item on an abductive basis: we remember the word 'burglar' and its previous interpretations relative to the actual facts of the story. Further, that solution is sustained by inductive inference from the rest of the story, for example that a TV and stereo are stolen supports the expectation that burglars typically are thieves. But, as noted already, as soon as the correct abductive inference is attained, we already know more than we needed to know in order to determine it sufficiently.

Item (3) is deductively linked (via syntax and semantics) to the burglar of item (2) and to the pronoun 'him' which appears as the second word before item (14), but can only be determined sufficiently by memory or by the inductive inference apparently made by Suzie that burglars are usually males. The fact that Suzie inferred that this particular burglar, entered alone, is sustained only by deduction from the use of 'him' in this cloze exercise. What her basis for such an inference might be is hardly germane to the text at hand. It can only be guessed at in any event. However, the determination of the correct answer 'he' (for item 3) will probably be based on the recollection (abductively understood) that Suzie only referred to one burglar in telling her story and that she actually referred to him with the pronouns 'he' and 'him'. And so it goes throughout the task.

It is easy to see that if we moved our starting point (the position of item 1) one word to the left, we would get a whole new set of cloze items, a different cloze exercise:

(II)   Hi. My name (1) —— Suzie. On Saturday night, (2) —— burglar broke into our (3) ——. He came through a (4) ——. He stepped right across (5) —— baby brother's crib. My (6) —— was asleep. He didn't (7) —— up. Everyone else was (8) —— too. I was asleep. (9) —— grandmother was asleep. My (10) —— was asleep. The burglar (11) —— the TV and stereo (12) —— went right out the (13) —— door. Nobody saw him, (14) —— we figured out what (15) —— the next morning.

By moving the starting point again one word to the left, we get still another cloze exercise:

(III)   Hi. My (1) —— is Suzie. On Saturday (2) ——, a burglar broke into (3) —— apartment. He came through (4) —— window. He stepped right (5) —— my baby brother's crib. (6) —— brother was asleep. He (7) —— wake up. Everyone else (8) —— asleep too. I was (9) ——. My grandmother was asleep. (10) —— mother was asleep. The (11) —— took the TV and (12) —— and went right out (13) —— front door. Nobody saw (14) ——, but we figured out (15) —— happened the next morning.

Since we started with an every fifth word deletion technique in constructing our first cloze exercise, two more exercises are possible:

(IV)   Hi. (1) —— name is Suzie. On (2) —— night, a burglar broke (3) —— our apartment. He came (4) —— a window. He stepped (5) —— across my baby brother's (6) ——. My brother was asleep. (7) —— didn't wake up. Everyone (8) —— was asleep too. I (9) —— asleep. My grandmother was (10) ——. My mother was asleep. (11) —— burglar took the TV (12) —— stereo and went right (13) —— the front door. Nobody (14) —— him, but we figured (15) —— what happened the next (16) ——.

(V)   (1) ——. My name is Suzie. (2) —— Saturday night, a burglar (3) —— into our apartment. He (4) —— through a window. He (5) —— right across my baby (6) —— crib. My brother was (7) ——. He didn't wake up. (8) —— else was asleep too. (9) —— was asleep. My grandmother (10) —— asleep. My mother was (11) ——. The burglar took the (12) —— and stereo and went (13) —— out the front door. (14) —— saw him, but we (15) —— out what happened the (16) —— morning.

It will become obvious to anyone who works through such a series of cloze exercises that individual items in them may differ markedly in difficulty. It will be equally apparent that the sort of preparatory experience that can be provided in a classroom setting can help to even out some of these differences across items from exercise to exercise. Prior experience with the facts and with the text on which the cloze exercises are based will make some of the more difficult items manageable (e.g. item 8 of cloze exercise I, 'too', and item 8 of IV, 'else'). The word 'too' is difficult to guess because it redundantly marks the agreement of the fact that other people were asleep with the fact that Suzie's baby brother was also asleep. Because of its redundancy, that is that the information it expresses can be deduced from other explicit statements of the text, 'too' could be omitted with little loss in information. Redundant elements of this sort are sometimes very difficult to guess because they express facts already obvious and are therefore not needed. The text may seem complete without such an addition. The word 'else' (item 8 of exercise IV) is also a difficult one to guess for essentially the same reasons. However, it is syntactically required by the appearance of 'too' later in the same sentence. Therefore, it can be inferred deductively by any examinee who is sufficiently sensitive to this subtle requirement of English syntax. However, few first-graders are apt to be that sensitive and probably no non-native speakers of English (at the first grade level) who are also trying to learn to read can be expected to know this connection by deduction. Hence, for them item (8) of exercise IV will be next to impossible unless they are given some experience with the text beforehand. In that case, if appropriate experience is provided, they may remember the use of the words 'else' and 'too' and they may be able to figure out their pragmatic connections with the facts of the story and later their syntactic/semantic relations to each other.

Cloze exercises like I–V are called open-ended because the examinee must supply the missing words, and the ones illustrated here are the most commonly used type of fixed-ratio exercises. In the examples provided, the ratio is one to five. That is, out of every five words, the fifth must be guessed by the examinee. It is also possible to delete the words on a variable ratio basis. Many such exercises could be derived from 'The Burglary' discourse in the form we have been working with. For instance, in exercise VI, the words that are omitted are all nouns.

(VI)   Hi. My (1) —— is Suzie. On Saturday night, a (2) —— broke into our (3) ——. He went through a (4) ——. He stepped right across my baby brother's (5) ——. My (6) —— was asleep. He didn't wake up. Everyone else was asleep too. I was asleep. My (7) —— was asleep. My (8) —— was asleep. The (9) —— took the (10) —— and (11) —— and went right out the front (12) ——. Nobody saw him, but we figured out what happened the next (13) ——.

Many other exercises of the variable ratio type are possible, but all of them together can add little or nothing to the full range of exercises of the fixed ratio type for any given fixed ratio.

Two basic methods for scoring open-ended cloze tests are commonly used. The simplest method is to count as correct only those answers that are identical to the words actually deleted in the construction of the task. This method is called *exact word* scoring. Another approach is to count any word as correct that fits the entire context. For instance, in exercise VI, for item (5), the word omitted was actually 'crib', but 'cot', 'bed', 'basket', or 'bassinet' would all be appropriate to the textual context and even to the facts as we understand them. The method of scoring just described is called *appropriate word* scoring. Both methods require some judgement. By the exact word method the response of each examinee must be compared with the original word. Usually spelling errors are ignored in most testing applications, but changes that result in a grammatically or lexically unacceptable variation are generally marked wrong. By the appropriate word method, the offered response, must be judged against the scorer's understanding of the intended meaning of the entire context. While the strictest variant of exact word scoring can be done by computer software, provided the answers are typed into an appropriate medium, appropriate word scoring generally requires a human scorer.

One way around the scoring difficulties of open-ended cloze items is to replace each blank with a list of alternatives in a multiple-choice format, as shown in VII below.

(VII)

	A. sister	
	B. name	
Hi. My (1) ——	C. mother	is Suzie. On Saturday (2) ——
	D. granny	
	E. baby	

A. afternoon		A. his	
B. morning		B. its	
C. night	a burglar broke into (3) ——	C. their	apartment. He
D. at noon		D. her	
E. at daybreak		E. our	

	A. tree		A. his
	B. hallway		B. its
came through a (4) ——	C. wall	He stepped right across (5) ——	C. my
	D. window		D. her
	E. mirror.		E. our

baby brother's crib. . . .

While multiple-choice cloze exercises require much more work to prepare, research shows that they measure many of the same kinds of abilities as the open-ended variety of tests. Their usefulness in large-scale testing is well established. However, because of the extra effort involved in the construction of such tests, they are less useful as day-to-day classroom activities.

More complex translation or translation-related tasks

In order to assess the more abstract kinds of deductive inference, open-ended questions (to be answered either orally or in writing), multiple-choice questions requiring inferences of a deductive or inductive sort (reading between or beyond the lines), summary tasks, or other interpretative tasks are required. All of these – including the tasks recommended above – it turns out, end up requiring some form of translation-type activity. We have already seen how the foregoing tasks involve the mapping of one form of representation (e.g. one uttered by the teacher) into a different form (e.g. one written by the student) by passing through a potential series of translations from the first surface form to any one of several underlying representations (e.g. sensory images, gestures, and abstract meanings) and eventually back to a different surface form.

It is equally apparent that paraphrase involves translation between distinct representational forms. For instance, in paraphrasing the sentence 'On Saturday night, a burglar broke into our apartment' Suzie might say 'Late on Saturday, while it was dark, someone jemmied the lock on a window of our apartment and broke in'. The new version of Suzie's statement would convey much of the same information as the former version. It is a paraphrase of the former statement because both of them, at the surface, end up in the same language. Both are statements uttered in English. For this reason, many theorists hesitate to speak of paraphrase as involving translation. Yet, it clearly does in terms of the theory laid out in Figs 5.2 and 5.3 see pages 57 and 60. Suzie must begin by interpreting the surface form of the sentence 'On Saturday night, a burglar broke into our apartment' into a deeper logical representation corresponding to the facts. This factual representation is then interpreted back into a surface form in English distinct from the one with which Suzie began. Certainly, this process may occur in stages, even phrase by phrase perhaps, but even so it must still involve translation in just the sense defined. If some deeper logical representation constituting the likeness in meaning of the two surface forms were not posited, it is difficult to imagine how we could judge the one to be a paraphrase of the other at all.

All such interpretative processes that reach beyond mere rote memory (according to the theory advocated here, see Figs 5.2 and 5.3) involve translation across distinct representational systems in the sense just illustrated. For instance, if Suzie could draw a very good captioned series of pictures showing what happened, there might be a good correspondence in meaning between the pictures (together with their captions) and the two paraphrase statements of the previous paragraph. However, the pictures could not be said to be merely a paraphrase of either or both of the statements. The series of pictures would rather be a translation of those statements insofar as the pictures would represent essentially the same meanings (somewhat more richly) and in a distinct form. Note further that because of the peculiar character of icons (which pictures are), unless some symbolic captions are provided (e.g. in a linguistic form), the pictures will not determine any particular interpretation with respect to the narrative. For instance, we will have no way of knowing when the events occurred relative to our own or to Suzie's experience. Pictures (icons in general) do not come with determined dates or connections to persons or times other than the ones pictured. The actual dates of occurrence, times, and connections with unpictured elements, remain unspecified by the pictures.

A more difficult variety of translation would be for Suzie to tell her story in Spanish, or some other language, just as she told it in English. This we would call a *translation proper*. If Suzie also knew American Sign Language (or some other sign system of a deaf community), she might be able to more or less simultaneously interpret (translate) her narrative into a signed version while speaking English, Spanish, or some other language. However, 'simultaneous translation' (also known as 'interpretation') is perhaps the most difficult sort since it requires a fluent switching between distinct languages in addition to all the other normal interpretative (translation) processes that must accompany the production or comprehension of discourse in any single language. Apparently simultaneous translation, and production in the second language, is actually done in the natural pauses of the producer of the original discourse. For this reason, the shorter the pauses and the more fluent the original discourse, the more difficult the translation task. It is probably the case that, in ordinary interpretation of any kind, working up the scaffolding necessary to the interpretation or production of discourse requires time. It can never be quite instantaneous.

It follows from strict logic that coming up with images (visual, auditory, tactile, olfactory, or gustatory), actual or imagined kinesic forms (e.g. bodily and facial gestures), imagined written forms, inferences, or any sort of judgements of discourse at all, must take time. No matter how fluent we are, we cannot generate speech (much less writing) instantly in correspondence to an observed series of events or any other form of meaning. Even the interpretation of sensory-motor images cannot occur instantaneously. In inventing a story (as opposed to retelling one, or recounting actual experience), the person producing the story must conjure up not only the images and inferences necessary to its interpretation but also must plan the very sequence of events itself, their integration, their reason for being (i.e. the motivation for the story), and probably a great deal more. Otherwise, if the story were merely a string of grammatical sentences invented off the top of someone's head, it could not be expected to make much sense, or even if it did make any sense, it would not likely be sufficiently well-motivated to capture the interest of many would-be listeners or readers. At any rate, because meaningful interpretations always involve the conversion of some form of representation into some other, every interpretation *is* an act of translation in the sense argued by our theory.

Open-ended tasks can be made easier (from the examinee's point of view) by putting them into a multiple-choice form where the examinee does not have to construct the discourse forms but merely to choose from several alternatives the one that best fits the fact(s). For instance, multiple-choice questions based on 'The Burglary' narrative might include the following:

(VIII) 1. The person telling the story is ——.
    (a) a little girl
    (b) an old woman
    (c) a small boy
    (d) a grown man
    (e) a busy housewife

2.   The story is mainly about a ——.
    (a) broken window
    (b) sleepness night
    (c) Saturday night party
    (d) baby in his crib
    (e) theft late at night

3.   The burglar in the story did *not* ——.
    (a) harm the sleeping infant
    (b) steal the television
    (c) take the stereo set
    (d) go out the front door
    (e) come in through a window

Each of the foregoing questions concerns facts actually known through abduction or deduction. Here are a couple of questions that can be answered from inductions based on linking the facts of the narrative with prior and possible future experience:

4.   The burglar will probably —— the TV and stereo.
    (a) keep
    (b) throw away
    (c) sell
    (d) take apart
    (e) return

5.   Suzie and her family were probably —— by what happened.
    (a) very pleased
    (b) pained
    (c) puzzled
    (d) annoyed
    (e) unsettled

Obviously, all such questions could be made easier or more difficult in a variety of ways. In general, however, all else being equal, deductive inferences determined by the semantics or syntax of the discourse will probably be more difficult for persons who do not know the language while inductive inferences will be more difficult for persons who do know the language. For persons who do not know the language, and therefore, who may have trouble understanding any question and its connection to facts, inductive inferences will be next to impossible. Provided adequate exposure to the facts is given via comprehensible representations, abductive inferences ought to be easier than deductive or inductive ones both for native speakers and for non-natives. However, the abductive connections between discourse and experience will be easier for persons who already know the language (and its various surface forms in speech and writing) than for persons who do not. In fact, persons who know the language and its various forms (spoken and written) very well will be able to access facts fluently and with relative ease from discourse alone without other scaffolding. However, in language and literacy programmes we are usually working with children who have not yet attained such an advanced stage of learning. As a result, scaffolding is critical.

In addition to multiple-choice tasks of the types just illustrated in items (1)–(5) of exercise VIII, a great multitude of tasks requiring more or less production of discourse (whether spoken, written, or some combination of these) can be conceived. In all such cases, ranging from open-ended questions at one end, through short-essay or (orally answered) questions, to creative writing and other interpretative tasks, according to the theory advocated here, the starting point for all such activities must be the actual facts of someone's experience. Leave out this element and the task, no matter what it might be, will tend towards meaninglessness. As a result, if the facts are left out or insufficiently determined, the performance of the task in question will be difficult to grade (whether by scaling or by scoring). It will, in short, be both unreliable and also invalid. Validity (according to the theory advocated here) depends on the linking of the discourse task to some relatively well-determined factual basis.

Under numeral IX several test types are listed roughly in an order of increasing difficulty:

(IX)   1. Open-ended questions presented orally for oral response.
       2. The same as (1) but with a written response.
       3. Same as (1) or (2) except that questions are in written form for short-essay type response.
       4. An oral summary of a fact-based discourse.
       5. A written summary.
       6. Expansion of the discourse in oral or written form (for instance,

telling what came before, after, or expanding the detail of some element in the fact-based discourse).
7. Paraphrasing or re-telling (oral or written).
8. Inventing a similar discourse based on one's own experience.
9. Writing such a discourse.

Some might object that the foregoing descriptions of tests must be based in a particular (simple) narrative, or at best a narrative-type task. This is no criticism. The fact is that all meaningful discourses of any type, to the extent that they are the least bit comprehensible or meaningful, relate ultimately to the ongoing stream of experience which is exactly like a narrative. For instance, consider a particularly abstract sort of discourse that is removed from ordinary experience. Consider a mathematical proof such as the proof of the Pythagorean theorem (that the sum of the squares of the sides of a right-angle triangle are equal to the square of the hypotenuse), or the proof that the square root of 2 is an irrational number. If these proofs or any other had no connection whatever to conceptions pertaining to practical experience (e.g. to our perceptions of triangles, their sides, and so on, our ideas about lines and squares and points on lines), it would merely be incomprehensible. In fact any mathematical proof, to the extent that it is understood at all, must be related to conceptions that in some degree relate to conceptions, objects, and events in ordinary experience.

Take another non-narrative sort of text such as a dictionary definition of a word. Say the word is an esoteric word such as 'otiose'. From the dictionary we determine that it may mean (1) 'at leisure, indolent, idle', or (2) 'ineffective or futile', or (3) 'superfluous or useless'. Someone might ask how such a dictionary entry (which we might well want to test at some point) can be related to any narrative. But suppose the word is encountered in the course of reading a certain book by a certain author. It is read on a particular occasion while riding a train from Albuquerque, New Mexico to Barstow, California, in the context of a certain essay by John Dewey on the character of intelligence which is said not to be 'an otiose affair'. As soon as some of the details of the experience that make the dictionary entry useful are added into the picture, we see that any such discourse genre (if a dictionary entry may be considered such) must always relate to some stream of experience with many connections that are exactly like those of a narrative. There is no difference with an encyclopedia entry, or a description in a catalogue, a parts manual, and so on. All such elements of discourse are utterly useless (and meaningless) except for their connections to the experience of persons who construct and use such reference materials in respect to actual experience. All such discourse elements have a narrative basis or they have no basis at all.

Therefore, it must be the case that every conceivable type of fact-based discourse (plausible fictions included) is more or less testable with essentially the same techniques as we have described above relative to our simple narrative about the burglar. If other genres of discourse are introduced in factual settings that are relevant to the experience of the children or are made relevant through some experience that the children in the classroom can identify with and understand, there is no limit to the kinds of language and literacy tasks that can be tested (and taught). Advertisements, menus, product labels, manufacturer warranties, and so on, can all be introduced within the fact-based contexts of meaningful experience. In such contexts, many of the above test-types can easily be extended to such discourse genres and no imaginable discourse-type (with any sort of experiential connections) will be even partly excluded from the kinds of tests recommended above.

Consider, for example, some of the kinds of spin-off activities and discourse genres that might be developed from the simple example narrative in our hypothetical 'big book', 'The Burglary'. What, for instance, would Suzie's mother and grandmother be likely to do after their apartment has been burgled? This question could itself be put to the children. (It requires an inductive generalization.) Suzie's family might well call the police and later file a report concerning the burglary. The telephone conversation (a dialogue) and the subsequent taking down of the facts for the written report would relate precisely to the facts of the burglary. The phone call, the subsequent interview between the mother (possibly grandmother), and the police might be dramatized, written down, and used as a dialogue (conversational) basis for a whole series of teaching and testing activities. The written report, of which a facsimile might be constructed as an addition to our big book, would itself provide a new discourse genre for expanding the literacy curriculum. It would have to contain detailed descriptions of the stolen items. We would need to find out the brand names, the manufacturers, and the approximate value of the TV and stereo.

Here, the question of whether the family or the landlord are covered by insurance might be raised. Such a question could lead Suzie's mother to call the landlord that owns the building to report the break-in and to urge him to repair the broken window and to improve the security of the building. Again this new dialogue could be used as a supplement to the curriculum already developed so far. It might be dramatized, written down, illustrated, taught, tested, and so on. But suppose the landlord is uncooperative? Should Suzie and her folks consider moving? They might want to check newspaper advertisements to see about other apartments. Did they have any insurance coverage to replace the stolen items? If so, a call to their insurance agent would be in order and could again expand the available discourse. A claim would have to be filed with the insurance company. But suppose that moving would be too expensive for them even to consider it. Maybe they ought to form a neighbourhood watch programme. This could lead into matters concerning laws that protect the property of citizens, how those laws are made, what crime costs, and so on. Many other genres of discourse might be introduced. Relative to the insurance claim, the replacement value of the stolen goods would have to be determined. The whole economic question could be brought into the picture along with countless other discourse possibilities. Moreover, because all of these potential expansions of the starting discourse relate to actual facts of experience (or plausible fictions that have such ties), all of the above recommendations concerning tests apply to all such forms of discourse.

Generally, for classroom purposes, when tasks of the sort described above in exercise IX are used, some general scale of adequacy supplemented by specific scales or diagnostic treatments of test performances will be preferred over a strict scoring procedure. For instance, the sort of scale recommended above (p. 74) might be used though it would have to be made a little more general in certain respects and more specific in others. Imagine, for example, that the task set (the test or teaching exercise) involves playing the role of Suzie's mother and responding orally to questions put by the police officer (a role, say, played by the teacher) taking a report about the burglary. Suppose further (just for the sake of the discussion here) that it has been previously determined that the date of the robbery was 2 November 1991, the TV was a 24-inch Sony worth about $450, and the stereo was a Panasonic that cost $650 when it was new. Imagine further that the children have read aloud, written from dictation, and participated in other activities in the classroom that would assure that the task at hand is not beyond what they might be expected to do with some success. Any unfamiliar information, or facts the children might not be expected to remember could be written on the board to be referred to as appropriate during the exercise. For instance, Suzie's address and telephone number might be put on the board along with the specific date of the crime, and the estimated cost of the TV and stereo. Suppose, finally, that the children are to write their responses to each of the following questions put by the teacher (acting in the role of the police officer):

(X) Now, Ms Doe, I understand that someone broke into your apartment and took some things. What is your address here?
What is your phone number?
Exactly when did this happen?
Okay. How did the person get in?
What things did he take?
I see. And about how much would you say the stolen items were worth?
Did he take anything else? Or was anyone harmed?

Notice that the questions asked in X (and in all tests or teaching activities that conform to the theory recommended here) must focus on the actual facts of the discourse activity. We do not ask about anything unrelated to what actually occurred. We do not invite students to invent sentences or any other sort of discourse detached from the facts of experience. We might want to include activities in the curriculum and in our testing where children give their own addresses or write their own stories, but in all such cases, the setting-up of such discourse events would pertain to particular well-determined facts. Also, the questions to elicit the various addresses and phone numbers of the several children, for instance, would be different in critical respects from the ones asked here. In exercise X, question (1) concerns the address where the burglary occurred. Just any old address or telephone number will not do. Similarly, question (3) concerns when the burglary occurred. Therefore, 12 October 1985, is not a correct answer. And so on, throughout. It is only because there are some determined facts upon which the discourse is based that the discourse itself has any particular meaning and that meaning is the only sufficient basis for the valid scalability (or scorability in other cases) of the task in question. Because the task pertains to relatively well-determined facts, responses *can be* scaled.

That is, responses can be judged for different degrees of accuracy to any desired level of detail. For instance, all the questions might be judged on a single five-point scale where, say, '5' means that all the requested information was provided and in a correct form, '4' means that nearly all the facts were conveyed in a correct or nearly correct form, '3' means that most of the facts were conveyed but with several errors in form, '2' means that some of the facts were conveyed but with some multiple errors, and '1' means that little or none of the facts were correctly conveyed. Such a scale could be applied in a rough and ready manner to the questions under numeral X, or almost any of those listed above under IX. Or, the formal aspects of the discourse task (e.g. pronunciation or legibility, spelling, punctuation, word-usage, grammar) might be separated, to some degree, from each other and from the comprehensibility and factual accuracy with which the examinee conveys the intended or desired information concerning the known facts. (Remove the known facts, incidentally, and any performance whatever will become difficult or impossible to scale or to score in any way.)

Distinct scales for factual content and formal accuracy (e.g. spelling, punctuation, vocabulary) of the spoken or written discourse forms can easily be imagined along the lines of the general scale just exemplified. However, in almost any classroom situation separate ratings assigned to all of the conceivable components of any given discourse task would make no sense at all. The trouble is that there are too many components. Imagine assigning separate ratings for content, organization, comprehensibility, spelling, punctuation, capitalization, word choice, morphological form, and syntax. (Also, notice that any one of these categories can be split up into a number of sub-categories that might be graded separately.) So many ratings would hardly be manageable from any teacher's point of view and neither would they be interpretable from the child's perspective (or the parent's or anyone else's, for that matter). Whatever grades, ratings, or scores are assigned, they must be interpretable and relatively simple. Therefore, specific diagnostic feedback on performances is best provided in terms of the correct answers (whether the correction involves a change in the conveyed fact, or in the form in which it is conveyed) relative to the facts. This feedback can be as specific as the particular problems that arise in any given child's performance and will have far greater potential benefit for the child than any number of distinct ratings that require an advanced college degree to construct or interpret in the first place.

For example, suppose the child were to write his or her own address in response to the question about where the crime occurred. The tester (teacher) might point out that the child is on the right track, an address is required, but that it needs to be Suzie's rather than the respondent's: 'not your address, *Suzie's address*'. Such feedback will be interpretable by the child exactly in proportion to the degree that the facts of the discourse in question have been determined by the teaching and, more particularly, by that child. Remove those facts and any such feedback will itself become relatively meaningless. Spelling errors, punctuation errors, problems in syntax, morphology, or whatever, can all be satisfactorily dealt with on a case-by-case basis provided the discourse activity is based on sufficiently determinate facts. Furthermore, it should be clear that if the recommendations contained here are judiciously understood and followed, at any given juncture in the negotiation of the curriculum, success is so very nearly guaranteed that children will generally be getting things right on the first or second attempt at any given activity (test or teaching exercise). There will not be very many errors of any sort. We will be teaching and testing for mastery, relatively complete understanding and ability to manage each phase of discourse processing as we go along. Each aspect of processing will be secured in order to provide a scaffolding for the next aspect prior to our getting to it. Therefore, we will generally be expecting (and getting) nearly perfect performances as we advance towards mature literacy and all its benefits.

Concluding observations

In the final analysis, we will teach and test all of the discrete-point surface elements of phonology, graphology (spelling), morphology, lexicon (capitalization), syntax (punctuation), semantics (word meanings), pragmatics (communicative forms and functions of all sorts), and so on, but always in richly developed factual contexts where sufficient scaffolding is provided so as to ensure success. If the starting guidelines (see above) are strictly observed throughout all phases of teaching and testing, as Richard Walker and Saowalak Rattanavich have argued throughout this book, success in attaining literacy is virtually guaranteed for all the children. Some traditionalists will object that the bits and pieces of language should be separated at the start and provided in tiny bites apart from any particular facts of experience. These persons do not understand the character of discourse. However, all that they seek to achieve by breaking things down into tiny bits and pieces *can and will be achieved by the methods recommended here* and they cannot in principle be achieved at all by strict discrete-point approaches.

Instead of discrete-point tests of phonemic contrasts, sound-symbol correspondences, spelling, punctuation, and so on, we recommend pragmatic tests that are fully and determinately grounded in known facts of experience. Pragmatic tests, of the sort exemplified throughout this chapter, together with the kinds of teaching activities recommended throughout the book, are robust. Unlike discrete-point tasks that divorce linguistic forms from their experiential connections, pragmatic tests are not susceptible to spurious training effects. If scores or ratings improve on a rich pragmatic task, these improvements will generally reflect real growth in relevant proficiencies. The same is not guaranteed for any discrete-point test where improvement is often related only to that specific test and no other. Also, teaching to pragmatic tests has no bad consequences at all. In fact, it is almost guaranteed to have a positive impact on the curriculum. To improve scores on pragmatic tests, it is necessary to advance the actual proficiencies in question.

CHAPTER 7

Improving literacy teaching in developing countries

RICHARD WALKER and SAOWALAK RATTANAVICH

The size and nature of the problem

The figure most commonly given for the number of illiterates in the developing world is one billion. But the true figure must be much higher because reported literacy rates are usually just the percentage of the population that receives elementary schooling, and not all who attend primary school become literate. Whatever the true figure, the problem is an immense one.

The highest incidence of illiteracy is to be found in some of the most populous of the developing countries, such as Pakistan, Bangladesh, and India and the number of illiterates is actually rising. There is no sign of a solution to the problem.

Many of the developing countries have put a high priority on the achievement of universal literacy, with primary education their first priority and some of them have achieved a large increase in school enrolments. But very often, the degree to which increased enrolments have translated into a higher literacy rate has proved disappointing. Thousands of new schools, with many thousands of children attending them, are tangible evidence of progress towards universal education but the elimination of mass illiteracy is much more difficult and problematic than the achievement of universal school enrolment.

An obvious area of difficulty in expanding the provision for education is teacher training but there are also some countries, such as Thailand, that have reasonably well trained teachers in all parts of the nation and yet have whole regions where both the school retention rate and the literacy success rate are intolerably low.

It seems that countries with a large culturally diverse and predominantly rural population have a particularly difficult task. Over and above the obvious difficulties of building, staffing and maintaining schools, such countries usually have exceptional trouble in achieving a satisfactory success rate in literacy teaching. First-year drop-out rates of up to 75 per cent are reported in some South American countries. The proportion of pupils who, having begun school, stay there and succeed in learning to read and write is intolerably low across whole regions and among some particular segments of their population.

Then there are the 'invisible' drop-outs – those who stay at school, but give up on learning to read and write. Very low success rates are found in almost every country, in isolated rural areas, in city slums, and among groups with a first language or dialect different from the language of instruction.

Overall, something like half of the world's population is illiterate. Three-quarters of those illiterates are to be found in south and east Asia, and there are very large illiterate populations in other parts of the world. For these countries to achieve universal primary education will involve massive expenditure, but funding alone will not solve the problem. There is a need for some kind of educational breakthrough by which the success rate of literacy teaching is greatly increased.

A literacy programme for developing countries

Ideally, a literacy programme for schools in educationally difficult regions of developing countries should have the following characteristics:

1. *It should be inexpensive.* With assistance from international agencies, it may be possible to find the extraordinary short-term funding needed to build and equip schools, but the recurrent cost per student of books and other materials must be low enough to be affordable when very few parents can contribute to the costs of schooling.
2. *The teaching methodology should suit the widest possible range of children,* and the programme itself should be easily modified to suit different regions and minority populations.
3. *The teaching methodology should be uncomplicated.* In a developing country, a sizeable proportion of the teachers who are brought into new schools during a large-scale literacy campaign, will inevitably have minimal training but the methodology should be such that they can master it.
4. *The reading programme should relate strongly to everyday life.* Where there is widespread poverty, survival has a much higher priority than education and neither the authorities nor parents will be inclined to expend a large portion of scarce resources on literacy education, unless it will help to supply primary needs. Even in developing countries, educators often do not realize how much that consideration affects attitudes towards learning and teaching.

Moreover, when learning to read and write make little or no immediate difference to standard of living or life prospects, the school and the community find it easy to accept teaching and learning failure. On the other hand, if literacy brings immediate and obvious benefits, few will be content with a low success rate, as the social climate supports educational improvement.

5. Finally, *the literacy programme should bring rapid results.* Teachers who have seen the failure of repeated attempts to improve a poor success rate, come to believe that what they are doing is all that can be done. That acceptance of failure has to be quickly replaced by expectation of success and for that, proof will be required that the new programme is undoubtedly better than the old.

Some factors to be considered

Programme planning in developing countries must go beyond the normal bounds of programme development. It should certainly encompass teacher training and programme dissemination.

Besides the immensity of the task of upgrading teacher competence, administrators in developing countries face other difficulties that would seem insuperable to administrators in more affluent countries. The number of teachers for whom places can be found in institutions of higher education may be hopelessly small, and neither the teachers nor the government may be able to pay the fees to fill what places are available. Moreover, it is probably impossible to withdraw teachers from the schools for inservice courses, because of teacher shortage.

Inservice teacher training seminars and workshops may be conducted in local centres during school vacations but that is usually expensive and difficult to organize, because of isolation and lack of transport. The best that most teachers can hope for is 'on-the-job' training, with a great deal of the responsibility for teacher inservice education being placed on local supervisors or advisers. The information that these people bring to teachers is likely to be specific to a programme or to a project and it usually has an administrative rather than an educational focus. As such, it does very little to deepen understandings of teaching or to encourage initiative.

When a new and very different literacy programme is to be instituted in schools, these factors restrict what can be done within the implementation plan. The nature of the existing school programmes, the degree to which the teaching and testing is centrally prescribed, the extent of cooperation that is available from local educationists and administrators, and what arrangements may be made with them for teacher inservice training all have to be explored, and current support and supervision systems need to be exploited to the full.

If there is to be the required level of systematic support and supervision, the new programme and methodology should be disseminated at all levels in the educational structure: from officials in the central office of education to individual teachers in the schools. And when a programme is being spread from one educational region to another, a choice has to be made as to whether indoctrination will begin with classroom teachers and work up to senior administrators or the reverse, or even to work from top down and bottom up, at the same time.

Because the Thailand operation was so large and diverse, covering the disparate regions of a large nation, what worked there should be well worth considering for at least some other developing countries. Because of this, here we present an account of programme development, teacher training and programme dissemination for CLE reading programmes in Thailand.

Developing a CLE literacy programme

The first systematic trial of a Thai-language CLE programme was carried out in 1987, in two isolated schools in Surin province, near the Kampuchean border. Some 60 per cent of the people of Surin province speak Khmer, 20 per cent speak Lao, 15 per cent speak other minority languages or dialects and only 3 per cent speak standard Thai, as their first language. Language difference and poverty are the reasons most often given for the fact that the literacy teaching success rate is low.

Two Grade 1 teachers in each of the two trial schools were inducted into CLE teaching over a period of four days after which they began teaching a Grade 1 CLE programme, using prototype teacher and pupil materials that the project team had brought with them. Further programme units were developed in subsequent weeks, and they were delivered and explained to the teachers as members of the project team made periodic follow-up visits to the schools.

After six months, an on-site evaluation of the pilot project was carried out by Dr John Chapman, of the Open University, UK. He concluded that the experimental programme was undoubtedly achieving superior results and he recommended that the work be continued and greatly extended (Chapman, 1987). He confirmed the finding of Rattanavich and Walker (1990), a month earlier, that almost all the children in the CLE groups were already reading and writing.

A grant was then obtained from the Rotary Foundation of Rotary International 'to develop and implement an effective primary school literacy programme for Surin, Buriram, Srisaket and Chaiyaphum provinces, and to evolve a plan for disseminating it throughout Thailand' (Rotary International, 1987).

It is necessary to carry out a trial of this kind wherever introduction of a CLE programme is contemplated. It is more than just a means by which a central team trials programme units under field conditions: it brings local people into the decision-making, it assists the development of sound strategies for programme development, teacher training, and teacher support, and it provides a realistic basis for costing future work. When large-scale work is envisaged, as in this case, the employment of an external consultant and an external evaluator, also seems highly worthwhile.

The project schedule

Table 7.1 shows the schedule for the project in the four north-east provinces. The plan was to develop the programme for each grade level over one or two years, to trial its major elements in a small number of classrooms during the next year, to pilot the full grade-level programme in 100 classrooms during the following year, and then to help the provincial education authorities to spread it more widely in subsequent years.

Table 7.1 Schedule for programme development and dissemination: Srisaket, Surin, Chaiyaphum and Buriram. (Cumulative numbers of class groups in the programme.)

Year	Grade 1	Grade 2	Grade 3	Grade 4	Grade 5	Grade 6
1988	100	7	Develop	Develop		
1989	400	100	7	programme	Develop	
1990	800	400	100	7	programme	Develop
1991	1600	800	400	100	7	programme
1992	2000	1600	800	400	100	7

To enable students to remain in the CLE programme, once they had entered it, programme development would move up by one school grade level each year. On that basis, programme units for Grade 6, the final year of the primary school, would be trialled in the final (fifth) year of the project.

So the two 'experimental' schools in Surin became 'trial' schools for the large-scale project and a third trial school in the same school district was added. Programme units for each successive school grade continued to be trialled in those three schools for the next five years, one year ahead of their use in forty 'pilot' schools.

As the work moved up the school grades and out to a greater number of schools, its complexity increased. A comparison of the work schedules for 1988 and 1991 reveals something of that increase.

In 1988, the first of the five years of the main project, the schedule for the year was as follows:

1. decide upon the procedures and range of materials for Grade 3, and write programme units;
2. trial the Grade 2 programme in seven classrooms in the one province;
3. pilot the Grade 1 programme in 100 classrooms, in four provinces.

By 1991, the second last year of the project, the work schedule for both the Central project team and the Ministry's provincial offices of education had greatly expanded.

The Central Project team was scheduled to:

1. determine the procedures and materials for the Grade 6 programme and write a range of the programme units;
2. trial units of the Grade 5 programme in seven classrooms in the one province;
3. prepare prototype teacher-training materials for Grade 5;
4. pilot the Grade 4 programme in 100 classrooms in four provinces;
5. ˙revise the Grade 4 teacher-training materials;
6. train forty regional trainers in four provinces for Stage 2 (Grades 3 and 4);
7. print the Grade 3 classroom and teacher-training materials.

The provincial offices of the Ministry were to:

1. conduct 'extension teacher training' for 800 additional Grade 1 teachers, 400 additional Grade 2 teachers, and 300 additional Grade 3 teachers in four provinces;
2. provide year-long supervision and conduct periodic follow-up seminars for newly trained teachers in the four provinces.

Programme costs

The low cost of implementing and maintaining the Thai CLE programme undoubtedly contributed to the rapidity of its spread. A classroom kit that supplied the needs of some thirty students for a year cost US$50 (£25.90) and most of the kit was reusable. Consequently, the replacement cost was approximately US$15 (£8) per class group per year, a figure that was within the Ministry's budget for the existing programme.

Project leadership

Unreserved commitment and perseverance is required at all levels of leadership in any major curriculum project. As can be seen from the increase in the yearly work schedule for the Thai project, however, comparatively few leaders were needed to begin with, and there was time for a structured leadership development scheme to take effect as the workload increased. For the Thai project, there was a pre-planned leadership training system that worked very well.

As the main project began, three leadership groups emerged: a National Coordinating Committee, a Central Project team, and four Provincial Project teams. The National Coordinating Committee consisted of senior representatives of Rotary, of the Ministry of Education, of the Srinakharinwirot University, and of the Central Project team. It met annually, at the time when programme expansion for the next year was being planned. Between those meetings, it did not have an operational role.

The Central Project team consisted of University staff, officers from the Ministry of Education, and Rotary leaders in Thailand. Throughout the five years, this team carried immediate responsibility for coordination of all aspects of the project.

Key personnel from provincial offices of the Ministry of Education managed the project within their own provinces. That included making local arrangements for training and follow-up seminars, and for week-to-week administration and supervision of the work in the schools. When extension training began in the third year of the project, Regional teacher trainers also became available in each province.

Members of the Central team and of provincial teams received training, as part of the project schedule. Members of the Central team were given training in Australia, as well as in Thailand. Through that training they became familiar with current theory and practice in literacy teaching and literacy programme development.

Project leaders at the regional and provincial levels were trained in Thailand by members of the Central Project team, with the assistance of resource persons who were invited from other countries. Other regional and provincial key personnel, including the regional teacher trainers, were trained by members of the Central Project team.

As the programme spread to further regions of the country, officers who had been appointed by the Ministry of Education to oversee the work in each major region were given training within the project leadership training scheme and they were able to use the training materials and procedures that had been developed by the Central Project Team within the main project.

An external chief consultant, Richard Walker, worked mainly with the

Central Project team. He made annual visits to Thailand, and maintained communication with the Project Coordinator and the Rotary Project Chairman between those visits. He also organized the training of project leaders who were brought to Australia for that purpose. The need for his guidance progressively narrowed as the Central team put teacher training and materials development systems in place, and as the programme moved up through the school grades.

No member of any of the Thai Central Project team worked full-time on the project – even the Project Coordinator retained a reduced but still sizeable University teaching load. Consequently, the two contacts with the external consultant each year facilitated regular intensive reviews of progress and attention to emerging problems that may otherwise have been over-shadowed by other professional responsibilities. In particular, they were occasions for firming up procedures and planning the work for the year ahead.

The Project Coordinator, Saowalak Rattanavich, remained directly responsible for programme development throughout the project. She also had direct control of materials development and 'core' teacher training. Regional teacher trainers carried out the 'extension teacher training' (beyond the 100 'pilot' classes for each grade level) but they were prepared for that work by the Central Project team.

One of the consequences of that personal oversight by the Project Coordinator and other members of the Central Project team was control of the programme 'dilution' that often occurs during large-scale programme dissemination.

As extension teacher training grew in volume, the weight of responsibility for programme dissemination moved more and more towards the Ministry of Education, and the Provincial Offices of Education were able to work more autonomously because they now had competent regional teacher trainers.

The schedule that is shown in Table 7.1 laid down what had to be achieved each year in materials development, teacher inservice training, and programme dissemination.

Materials development

As the project began in February 1988, the Grade 1 programme was nearing the end of its 'trial' year. The Grade 1 programme materials were revised on the basis of that trial, and 100 copies of the starter books and the same number of classroom kits were assembled for the Grade 1 classes in the 'pilot' schools.

An instructional video was made from footage obtained in one of the trial schools and a prototype Stage 1 Teacher's Manual was prepared during the early months of 1988. These were reviewed later in the year, and they were heavily revised before they were produced in quantity for the third year. The same process was followed for Stages 2 and 3, in subsequent years.

A writers' workshop was held, in parallel with the last five days of the ten-day orientation seminar, to develop starter books for Grade 2. The people who were chosen to participate in that workshop were educators with known writing expertise, who had attended the orientation seminar during the previous five days in order to become familiar with principles behind the CLE programme. However, the books did not prove to be as satisfactory as was hoped, and the writers' workshops that were held in later years had a different format: the later workshops focused on instruction in book writing and on the specifications for the starter books. The books were then written in the writers' own time.

In every year after the first, the teacher's notes for the year of the programme that had been piloted were reviewed and revised by regional trainers as a part of their training. These notes were then copied in sufficient number for 'extension' training purposes.

The final version of the teacher training materials for Stage 3 (Grade 5 and 6) training was timed for production in the fifth year of the project, in time for use in other regions of the nation.

Strategies for teacher training

By the end of the fourth year, over 20,000 teachers had been trained in various parts of Thailand. This was achieved through what was called the 'multiplier strategy':

1. the Central Project team trained 200 teachers in pilot schools for each of the three stages of the programme;
2. in their second year of teaching, the most effective forty or so of these teachers were trained to operate as regional teacher trainers; and
3. from the third year, these regional teacher trainers staffed the teacher training seminars and follow-up sessions for hundreds of other teachers each year.

When regional trainers trained teachers, that was called 'extension training' as opposed to 'core' teacher training – the training of teachers in pilot schools, by the Central Project team. The materials for extension training were provided by the Central Project team but the Regional trainers played their part in developing those materials. For example, they reviewed and revised the teacher's manual and teacher's notes for their level of the programme, in the course of their training. Because extension teacher training seminars occurred in vacation time, regional trainers did not have to be withdrawn from their own (pilot) schools.

After the decision to spread the programme nationwide, the regional trainers also took part in spreading it to other regions, by special arrangement.

As the CLE programme was introduced into each province, a ten-day seminar was conducted to familiarize provincial and district administrators, provincial supervisors and district supervisors with the project, the programme, and the methodology, before the first teacher training began. At this seminar, these senior participants actually went through the teacher training sequence for the Grade 1 CLE programme shown in Fig. 7.1, before they planned the teacher-training and supervision programmes for their own province. The principals of pilot schools were also given an orientation seminar before the actual teacher training workshops took place.

There were several reasons for giving these senior people first-hand experience with the CLE teaching and teacher training before their teachers became involved. In these isolated areas of the country, it was highly desirable that the normal provincial, district and school support and supervision systems operate for the CLE programme and that they operate efficiently. Moreover, it was considered that the provincial administrators were most likely to develop a sense of ownership of the programme, and make better judgements for its further dissemination if they had a key leadership role, from the very beginning.

In the case of the original four north-east provinces, that leadership role was taken up immediately, as they went on to set up the training workshops for the Grade 1 teachers in their pilot schools straightaway. The teachers themselves were trained in separate nine-day seminars, at their own provincial centres. These teachers left the seminars equipped with the starter books, the classroom equipment, and the materials that they needed to teach for at least a month.

The teacher training strategy that is shown in Fig. 7.1 remained virtually unchanged throughout the term of the project in Thailand.

The training workshop begins with an introduction to the CLE programme and principles. The teaching of the first phase of a programme unit is then demonstrated with a group of children, and reviewed in group discussion. Then, those that are being trained teach that phase of a different programme unit to groups of other children, after which they reassemble to review their teaching of that phase. This procedure is repeated for each of the phases of the CLE teaching sequence, in turn.

Phase 4, which is the making of a 'big book' and preparing word cards, can be done overnight and Phases 1 and 2 may be combined, thereby

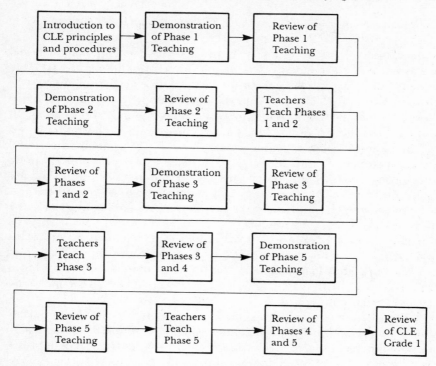

Figure 7.1: The Grade 1 CLE teacher-training sequence

reducing the number of demonstration and practice teaching sessions to three. Accordingly, the minimum length for a teacher-training seminar is three days but it was found desirable to use four days if that were possible. That minimum is set more by the needs of the students than of the teachers, because the groups of students must spend sufficient time on each phase to be able to participate adequately in the teaching of the next phase.

As was stated at the beginning of this section, the most successful Stage 1 teachers and supervisors were given additional training to enable them to act as regional trainers. In their first year of operation, the Stage 1 Regional trainers trained 300 Grade 1 teachers, with members of the Central Project team present, but not taking an active role. Over the next few years, regional trainers for each of the three Stages of the programme trained thousands of teachers, unaided by the Central team except for the supply of basic teacher and pupil materials.

Each year, however, the Central Project team trained and equipped 120 'core' teachers, who piloted the next higher grade level of the programme.

Programme dissemination

With the schedule for the five-year project being maintained, regional trainers trained 800 Grade 1 teachers, 400 Grade 2 teachers, and 300 Grade 3 teachers in 1991. By the end of that year, the Grade 1 programme was being taught in 1600 classrooms in the north-east provinces and some 650 classes in other parts of the land the Grade 2 programme was being taught in more than 1000 classes and the Grade 3 programme in over 400 classes.

Beginning two weeks after Grade 1 teaching began in the 'pilot' classes, members of the Central Project team visited every pilot school. They brought with them additional Grade 1 starter books, and they discussed with the teachers how they had handled the first programme unit and how they might implement the remaining programme units over the weeks ahead.

These initial follow-up visits to schools were regarded as important because they gave an early indication of how effective the first teacher-training workshops had been, and they enabled the project team to find out what was occurring as the programme was introduced across that range of school situations.

After that, the Central Project team revisited these schools at intervals of two months, and half-yearly meetings were held with participating teachers and administrators, to review progress and to discuss possible improvements and modifications. Follow-up visits to the Grade 2 trial classes were continued along with the school visitation programme for Grade 1.

The first end-of-year review, and a comparison of the test scores of the CLE students and a similar number of students still on the old programme, revealed that

1. the CLE Grade 1 programme was clearly producing better results than was the old programme, but that
2. future training workshops should lay greater stress on organizing a class-room for CLE work, and how to move towards teaching a class in small groups.

After 1988, the pattern for bi-monthly follow-up visits was changed so that all of the CLE teachers and supervisors of a province gathered at the provincial centre for a half-day discussion with members of the Central Project team twice each year. Following each of those meetings, Central Project team members visited schools that had been chosen by the provincial key personnel. The schools that Central Project team members visited were chosen as schools needing special help, schools where exceptionally interesting work was being done, and schools that had not been visited for some time. In addition, members of the Central Project team continued to visit the three trial schools.

This procedure was found to be more productive, now that the project team had become familiar with the environment of all the schools. Some advantages of the new system were that it:

1. facilitated administration of the whole project;
2. contributed to teacher morale through the sharing of ideas and experiences;
3. allowed wide-ranging discussion of important matters and an unhurried question and answer session; and
4. saved the project team a great deal of time that would otherwise have been spent in travelling to and from schools, repeatedly giving the same information.

The second year also saw the first 'follow-up meetings' for Grade 1 'extension' teachers that had been trained by Regional trainers. Members of the Central team who attended these first meetings as observers found them highly encouraging in that these teachers seemed in no way inferior to those who were teaching Grade 1 in the pilot schools.

As the CLE programme reached Grade 2 in the pilot schools, teachers began to feel pressure from provincial tests, because the province-wide examinations begin in that grade. Teachers sought reassurance that the results of their students in the provincial examination would not be lower than those who were using the conventional programme, which was designed to prepare them for that examination. Some teachers even tried to teach elements of the conventional programme as well as the CLE programme – a procedure that would certainly confuse their students.

This will commonly become a source of concern in the early stages of substituting a functionally oriented programme for one that is built on traditional sub-skills principles if the students still have to undergo testing that has a discrete-point, sub-skills orientation.

The trialling of the Grade 2 programme had shown that pupils who go through Grades 1 and 2 of the CLE programme develop sub-skills to a high level as well as being much more competent in higher-order literacy skills. That information was given to the Grade 2 teachers but they were also told that any doubt that their students would score well on sub-skills test could be dispelled by adding to Phase 5 of each programme unit games that were oriented towards the particular sub-skills.

To substantiate that advice, the project team administered both conventional and 'pragmatic' literacy tests to 25 per cent of the Grade 1 students and 48 per cent of the Grade 2 students who were in the CLE programme, and compared their results with those from testing a similar number of students from matched class groups outside the programme.

On the 'pragmatic' test items, the scores of CLE students were very much superior indeed – a high proportion of the 'control' group children failed absolutely to cope with many of those items. However, the main concern of the teachers was with scores on the standardized 'Thai language performance test', provided by the Thai Ministry of Education. On that test, the scores of the CLE student groups were also superior for both Grade 1 and Grade 2, with differences that were significant at the 0.001 level of confidence. These results on tests by which literacy achievement would be assessed in provincial examinations provided very welcome support for the reassurance that the project team had so often to give.

However, the use of discrete-point provincial examinations in literacy placed unnecessary stress on the Grade 2 CLE teachers and a request that students within the CLE programme not be required to sit for the current provincial literacy tests was endorsed by the Central Office of the Ministry of Primary Education and the problem was solved for that year.

However, the quality of literacy testing is of central importance in improving literacy curricula and literacy teaching because, as John Oller points out in Chapter 5, 'Curriculum and teaching will rise or fall to the level of the testing'. With an urgent need to improve literacy testing before the CLE programme was adopted nationwide, the Ministry of Education and the project team cooperatively mounted a national seminar and workshop on language testing, headed by John Oller. In the workshop, new schemes for language testing and new test instruments were planned and reports indicate that many of the provinces are continuing that work by setting up local training seminars in literacy testing.

Formative testing continued to reveal that rapid improvement in learning to read, write and speak Thai was occurring, in all areas where the programme was introduced. That kind of evidence remained strong after the Stage 2 programme was introduced – almost all Grade 3 and Grade 4 students could write lengthy reports, stories, poems, and others kinds of texts. This was a crucial outcome because everywhere, the real incidence of failure to learn to read and write seems to become evident at that stage of schooling.

In the fourth year, too, questionnaires were widely used to collect information on such things as student attitudes to school, to reading and to writing, and on teacher perceptions about the adequacy of CLE training, CLE teacher materials, and follow-up support. The data that was collected revealed clear gains in all these affective areas, even more so in the southern and northern provinces than in the north-east, where the project began.

Extension beyond the main project

Towards the end of the second year, 1990, it was decided to investigate whether the CLE programme should be introduced in the south of Thailand. Members of the literacy team visited the south of Thailand to see the educational conditions that existed there, and to prepare teachers in each province to teach the first three units of the Grade 1 programme, as a test of its effectiveness with children of these strongly Muslim communities where Yawee (a Malaysia dialect) is spoken as first language. It was found that:

1. in some schools, very few of the students, at any grade level, could speak standard Thai;
2. there was an appearance of severe poverty in rural families, though not so extreme as in the north-east provinces;
3. school attendance was poor;
4. particularly in rural schools, the majority of the students were failing to learn to read or write;
5. all the supervisors, principals, and teachers were enthusiastic at the prospect of using the CLE programme.

The trial with three Grade 1 programme units was highly successful, and all thirty-seven trial schools were equipped and trained to continue with the programme, as demonstration schools. The results from end-of-year testing in these schools are particularly interesting. Table 7.2 gives a comparison of the scores – on a 'cloze' test of reading, a writing task, and a dictation test – of the thirty-seven class groups that were on the CLE programme and an equal number of matched class groups that were on the conventional literacy programme. The performance of the students on the CLE programme was clearly superior on all three tests – at the 0.001 level of confidence.

Late in the same year, the Thai Ministry of Education informed the

Table 7.2 A comparison of Thai language scores of Grade 1 CLE programme students in the five southern border provinces and those in control classes for the 1990 academic year

Comparison of pilot and control Grade 1 classes Southern provinces 1990	CLE schools (37 classes)		Control school (37 classes)		
	X	SD	X	SD	t
Scores on cloze test of reading	9.99	7.87	5.28	6.37	13.64
Scores on writing task	13.90	10.16	9.79	10.63	8.17
Scores on dictation task	30.37	15.44	23.85	16.77	8.36
Total scores	54.26	25.45	38.92	25.62	12.39

p <0.001

project team that the CLE methodology for language and literacy teaching had been adopted for the nation in the Plan for National Economic and Social Development (1992–96). At the same time, the Ministry requested cooperation in quickly establishing a CLE programme in schools of the northern hill-tribe provinces, and in setting up demonstration schools in all other provinces, before 1992.

With the spread of CLE teaching to all regions of the land, the writing of 'regional' starter books became a priority. A book development workshop was held to produce starter books for use with hill-tribe students. More than thirty Grade 1 and Grade 2 books were produced for trial in those northern schools.

By the middle of the 1991 school year, some 350 hill-tribe schools were using the CLE programme in Chieng Mai, Mae Hong Sorn and Chieng Rai provinces. The programme was introduced simultaneously into Grade 1 and Grade 2 classes, to save a year in taking the programme up through the grades. That strategy involved using a condensed Grade 1/Grade 2 programme with the first Grade 2 groups, but that can be done because the learning–teaching strategies do not change substantially between those two grades.

Follow-up visits revealed that, unlike in the past, these students were now purposefully engaged in school learning at a rate comparable to students in other parts of Thailand, and they were speaking, reading and writing standard Thai in the course of their learning activities.

Further training seminars in six northern provinces catered for another 650 teachers before the end of 1991. It seemed that the number of schools that could begin CLE teaching was limited by the supply of classroom kits rather than by ability to provide teacher training or any lack of schools willing to change to the new programme.

Finally, thirty people who had proved to be highly successful in CLE teaching and teacher training were selected from all regions of Thailand to undertake a special role in the large-scale inservice teacher training that was planned for all regions of the country during the following and subsequent years. They received additional training in a six-day seminar/workshop.

Unrelated to preparation for the 1992–96 National Plan for Education, Thai-language preschool CLE work sprang up in preschool centres, ranging from centres in Bangkok slums to private preschool centres. The latter marked the first use of the CLE method by teachers in private schools.

Work with English-language CLE programmes

CLE teaching of English began on a small scale in primary schools in several provinces where the Thai-language CLE programme had been introduced. Teachers there used materials that had been developed by graduate students of Srinakharinwirot University during their practicum in teaching English. The results of the trial were encouraging, but it became clear that teachers needed much greater support if they were to teach English in English, rather than attempting to teach it in Thai.

During 1990, a CLE-training workshop was conducted for 120 teachers of English in Buriram and Chaiyaphum to explore further the possibility of teaching English as a foreign language, using CLE techniques. Some forty of those teachers abandoned the conventional Grade 5 English programme in favour of a CLE programme.

After these teachers had trialled CLE techniques for a year, the Ministry of Education decided to explore more widely the possibility of using CLE techniques in the teaching of English. The Central Project team, reinforced by a teacher from Australia, staffed a Ministry of Education seminar for 100 teachers of English from all provinces of Thailand. English-language starter books for Grade 5, with cassette audiotapes, and prototype 'English for CLE teachers' booklets, with accompanying audiotapes, were produced for the occasion.

Following that workshop, it was proposed that a complete programme and teacher-training materials for teaching English as a foreign language should be developed in Thailand for use there and in neighbouring countries. This project is still being formulated at the time of writing.

Conclusion

There is no doubt that CLE techniques are exceptionally effective for teaching literacy to children whose mother tongue differs from the language of instruction. Some CLE schools in Buriram province, for example, have only Khmer-speaking children, in other schools in Surin and Srisaket, there are both Khmer- and Lao-speaking students, and in still other schools, Lao is the predominant first language. In south Thailand, the mother tongue of almost all the children is a language that is a dialect of Bahasa Malaysia, a very different language from Thai.

But the most convincing evidence came from the northern provinces of Thailand. The schools of Chieng Mai province, for example, range from those where all the students speak an easily understood northern regional dialect of Thai to schools where all the students speak one or another of the hill-tribe languages that are incomprehensible to Thai speakers. After trialling the CLE programme across those differing situations, the Chieng Mai Office of Primary Education is now spreading the CLE programme through all its schools, as rapidly as resources allow.

Add to that the use of the CLE methodology with Australian Aboriginal children and with children in India and Bangladesh, and it can be said that the methodology has been tested across a wide range of language situations.

It is significant, too, that many of these children were from totally illiterate family backgrounds. The Australian Aboriginal children, most of the children in the rural areas of north-east Thailand, and all the hill-tribe children, came from homes that did not contain a single item of written material in any language.

The system for inservice teacher training that was developed in Thailand also appears to be a highly effective one for developing countries and, as such, it could prove very useful in other countries. The teacher inservice training task that faced the Thai Ministry of Education in changing their national literacy curriculum, seemed to be a huge barrier to instituting a better literacy programme.

But the procedures had been developed, the teacher training materials had been produced, and large numbers of teachers had been trained in every region even before the five-year plan was to take effect. And there seems to have been remarkably few teacher-training failures, even when teachers trained other teachers.

A third significant factor was the use of writers' workshops to adapt the programme to a new region. It was found that teachers and others could quickly be trained to write CLE starter books and unit outlines that were suited to the needs and characteristics of students in a particular region of the country.

An account of the rapid spread of a programme necessarily emphasizes mass teacher training and the mass production of materials. In doing that, it may give an impression that every CLE teacher, everywhere in Thailand, is teaching in exactly the same way, following the same teaching plans, and completing each programme unit in the same length of time. That impression is misleading, because no two classrooms are the same. In one classroom, there may be an atmosphere of noisy competition, with cheer squads in full cry while, in another, there will be quiet, concentrated activity, as small groups of students cooperate in pursuing their allotted tasks. Very different classroom practices have developed from an understanding of the same basic principles CLE teaching. Teachers realize that, as long as they keep to the CLE teaching sequence, there is more than ample scope for variation in teaching style, in group activities and in content.

There is ample room, too for teachers to be pedantic about spelling and good handwriting if they see that as necessary, provided that the sub-skills teaching is done in the final phase, using CLE procedures, and as long as competent students are not being unduly delayed or becoming bored.

Moreover, the range of games and other activities that have been invented by Thai teachers for the final phase of Stage 1 and Stage 2 CLE teaching is somewhat overwhelming to those who visit many schools because different ones are to be seen everywhere. What goes on in classrooms that are truly student- and activity-centred can be as varied as are the students themselves, and what they and their teachers enjoy doing.

Then there are the kinds of differences that occurred between the CLE programme units that were developed in Alice Springs for Aboriginal students, and those produced in Thailand. In the Alice Springs programme, for example, every programme unit tended to continue for a number of weeks or even months. The student texts there were more elaborately produced, with photographs and even drawings by professional artists, and with heavy, well-designed covers. In Thailand, although the orthography in the group texts tended to be more beautiful and exact, the students did all the illustrating, and after the first few months, they also wrote the script for their group texts.

Those differences stem from the local culture, from what technology is available, from different notions as to what students get from making a text, and from what further use will be made of it. Group texts are used continuously in areas of Thailand where there are few other reading materials, so that they fall apart by the end of the year. In contrast, the Alice Springs texts were preserved almost as show pieces. No doubt the group texts being produced by the children in India and in Bangladesh are different again.

To reiterate what was stated in Chapter 4: a CLE programme cannot be transported from place to place. Instead, every CLE programme should be developed where it is to be used, and, as far as possible, by those who will use it. That being so, CLE programmes will look different in the classrooms of different countries and peoples.

Finally, CLE programmes can be very inexpensive, once they have been fully developed so that they promise a timely breakthrough to achieving the cost-effectiveness that is needed if universal literacy is to become more than a dream in many of the developing countries. It is true that such an educational breakthrough is only a beginning to a full solution of mass literacy problems, hopeful though that is. For example, when Thailand has successful CLE school literacy programmes operating in all parts of the country, it will have created a further problem for itself: the schools will need well-stocked libraries for use by their actively literate students. To have reached this problem, however, is to have gone a long way down the road to alleviating mass illiteracy.

CHAPTER 8

Reflecting on the contexts of reading

RICHARD WALKER

Introduction

The central message of this book is that there is no need for so many children to fail to become active readers and writers – in either industrialized or developing countries. It was asserted in Chapter 1 that we should cease explaining away the sizeable proportion of children who fail to learn to read and write and, instead, devise school programmes through which *all* the students learn to read, not just those who have some particular kind of family and experiential background.

It follows that we should also critically examine all compensatory programmes. It is the nature of compensatory programmes that they require children, who are perceived to be different in some way, to travel by a different and usually longer road to literacy than do other children. This being so, we have to be quite sure that a compensatory programme is not just an attempt to change children so that they fit into the existing programme rather than to change the school programme so that it suits all the children.

To judge by a recent front-page report in the Australian national newspaper (*The Australian*, 29–30 June 1991), there are some who even want the compensatory programmes to include the whole family. Under the headline 'Illiteracy may be inherited' this feature article reports on a research finding that a high proportion of school children who are having reading difficulties have at least one parent who cannot read or write; and it goes on to state,

> There is strong evidence that illiteracy is an inherited trait, and some educationists believe it is a contagious disorder best cured by treating the whole family.

The article also reports that

> 30 per cent of the families admitted or were strongly suspected of at least two generations of illiteracy

but it does not suggest that the treatment extend back beyond the living.

People who reason from that philosophical basis would surely have recommended a compensatory language programme for Mary, the little Aboriginal girl who was described in Chapter 1; but Mary's later performance within the Traeger Park CLE programme proved that no compensatory programme was needed. She was a child of more than average potential, who did not need to be changed in any way before she was ready to learn to read and write. The fact that the CLE approach has subsequently succeeded with many thousands of children in many situations, where there had been a history of gross failure, indicates that Mary's is not an isolated case; and that there are many Marys in many places who are failing to learn to read and write only because the school literacy programme is failing them.

A note about contexts

Associated with that central message, and with how the number of failures may be reduced, several major sub-themes permeate what all three authors have written. One such sub-theme is a need to abandon language-reading programmes that focus only on the phonological and the syntactic levels of language, apart from context and purpose. To quote John Oller from Chapter 7, 'A certain recipe for failure in any kind of language instruction is to get children to process linguistic forms that are essentially unrelated to any factual data.' It is from the context of reality – of human needs and daily life – that the meaning, power and usefulness of language is derived; and to try to teach language as if it can be isolated from context is a nonsense.

This chapter presents a closer examination of that sub-theme; and its implications for literacy teaching.

There are two types of context:

1. the context to which the language refers; and
2. the context in which the students are operating.

For convenience, we shall refer to the first of these as the *referential context,* the context to which the language refers; and the second kind as the *operational context,* the situation within which the language users are operating. As quoted above, Oller is referring to both of those kinds of contexts, but some elaboration is still needed.

When a class in a school in England is talking about hunting deer in the Appalachian Mountains of the United States of America, their operational context is their English classroom, its occupants and what is going on there. At the same time, their referential context – what they are talking about – is hunters, deer, the terrain of the Appalachian Mountains, and what goes on there.

In CLE teaching, there is an exceptionally strong focus on the operational context, because, in difficult educational circumstances, the first priority is to develop learning/teaching environments that enable all the students to become actively involved. Only when that has been done, can the teacher focus on managing those environments in ways that enable the students to engage in discourse, and thereby to learn to use language.

The process of 'scaffolding', that has often been mentioned in previous chapters, depends on context – it amounts to contextual support. When discourse relates to and is supported by non-linguistic cues, and when it relates to what Oller refers to in Chapter 5 as 'facts of experience', it is said to be *scaffolded*.

Those facts of experience have to do with the referential context as defined above. However, discourse has structure and function on a deeper level than the meaning of linguistic items. In real life, discourse occurs in the course of and is intermeshed with interactive non-language activity. All important types of interactive activity has structure and real-life purposes; and participants need to understand what is going on, and how what is being said relates to other aspects of what is going on, if they are to manage their part in the discourse. This has to do with the operational context of the discourse.

Fig. 8.1 shows spoken discourse as being related to both a referential context and an operational context. It could be said that the language used in the discourse derives its meaning from its referential context, and its function and purpose from its relationship to the operational context. Those two contexts may or may not be the same.

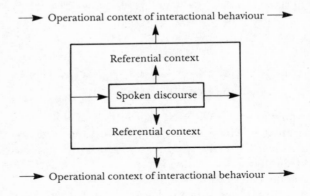

Figure 8.1: Spoken discourse related to both a referential and an operational context

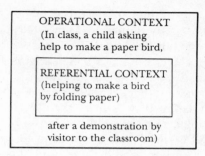

Figure 8.2: Coincidence of referential context and operational context

The task of language users is easiest when the referential context and the operational context coincide, so that they are talking about what is going on around them.

Fig. 8.2 illustrates this kind of situation. A Japanese visitor has shown a class of children how to fold paper to make a bird and flap its wings; and a student is asking another for help to make such a bird. Under these circumstances, the amount of information that has to be included in the child's request is minimal, because the referents (the task, the paper, the bird that the visitor has made, and the child who is addressed) are visible to both children, and both have witnessed a demonstration of the required process (folding the paper). The child would say something like, 'Help me to make my bird.'

When the referential context coincides with the operational context, the chances of being misunderstood are close to zero – so much so, that the request would very likely be understood even if the second child could not speak the language, the more so if facial expression, intonation and gesture are taken into account.

Another way of looking at this is shown in Fig. 8.3. The language behaviour is interwoven with and is interpretable against non-language behaviour, and, at the same time, the talk is about objects and people that are present and visible. In these circumstances, learners can easily and confidently relate language elements to corresponding elements and rela-

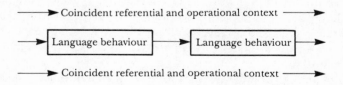

Figure 8.3: Language behaviour related to a context of non-language behaviour

tionships of the reality being spoken or written about – the language interaction is heavily scaffolded – and they also know what speakers are trying to
achieve by their talk, and how the language interaction fits into what else is
going on. The resemblance to what is happening as an infant begins to
understand and speak its mother tongue is obvious.

Let us suppose, however, that a day has passed and the child who made
a paper bird has to recount that event to the class (still within the classroom). The child's language task would now be more difficult; and more
complex language will be needed to carry it out. But the increase is not
great because the paper bird is still there, and the listeners have also
witnessed the events that are being recounted. The child might say something like, 'Harry and I made that paper bird, yesterday, after the Japanese
lady showed us how.' That would be enough to recall the experience,
together with memories of associated circumstances and events; and further talk about what happened, who did what, and personal reactions to all
and any of those things could readily flow.

However, let us imagine that the recounting took place away from the
classroom. In the absence of what is being spoken about, there is a greater
possibility of misinterpretation, so more information has to be given and
the language task becomes more difficult again. The child would have to
say something like, 'Did you see the paper bird that Harry and I made at
school yesterday, after the Japanese lady showed us how?' Nevertheless, it
would not be difficult for the listeners to relate that to the actual events.

But suppose, instead, that the child is recounting that same event to
her mother, who did not witness the paper-folding event. Now the task is
considerably more difficult and the language has to convey considerably
more information about the referential context. With all efforts, the referential 'reality' that the mother builds up in her mind will differ from what
actually occurred, the more so if she has never personally experienced such
an event.

The child may have to say something like, 'A Japanese lady came to
school yesterday, and she showed us how to make a bird out of paper.
Harry and I made one, and we could even make it flap its wings like hers
did.'

In the circumstances that are illustrated in Fig. 8.4, the mother has to
draw inferences from her own experience of school-room situations and
paper-folding to fill out a picture from what the child is saying. And complex discourse skills and relatively complex language may be called upon,
in questions and answers, before the participants are satisfied that they fully
understand each other.

The gradation in difficulty that we have sketched out for spoken discourse applies also to written language tasks, revealing an important dimension of what makes some reading and writing tasks harder than others.

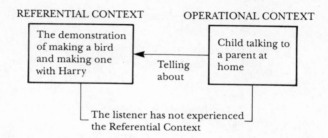

REFERENTIAL CONTEXT   OPERATIONAL CONTEXT

The listener has not experienced
the Referential Context

Figure 8.4: Referential context unrelated to the context of operation

The task for readers and writers is least demanding when the referential context coincides with the operational context, as in Fig. 8.2. In those circumstances, what is being written or read is readily interpretable against the reality to which it refers, whereas, in the circumstances that are shown in Fig. 8.4, the task may well be impossible if the reader has not had experience with the referential context.

A child's first encounters with written language should be amidst a context of shared experience, with the written language being open to clear interpretation and discussion because it refers to that shared context. To a considerable extent that explains why the strategies that are used in Phases 1 and 2 of the Stage 1 CLE programmes enable all the students to participate in the learning. If, on the other hand, the first experience that children have with reading resembles the situation shown in Fig. 8.4, the chances are high that some of the children will not be able to understand what is going on, in the absence of strong contextual support for the language.

When the language of instruction is a second language or second dialect

Another sub-theme of this book has been that children can learn to speak a second dialect or second language along with learning to read and write. The more general policy has been to introduce the students to the written mode of a language only after they have a reasonable grasp of the spoken mode; so that instruction in the speaking of the language of instruction precedes learning to read and write. As was pointed out in the conclusion to Chapter 7, experience with CLE programmes casts serious doubt on the necessity for that. It seems very likely that young children are more capable language learners that they are given credit for by those who see a need for teaching only one language mode at a time.

If we continue our examination of scaffolding, in terms of contextual support for language, we can see why that may be so.

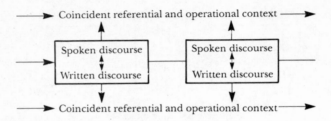

Figure 8.5: Spoken and written discourse, related to each other and to the same contexts

Fig. 8.5 shows corresponding spoken and written language being used along with the non-language contexts behaviour that they refer to, as happens in Phase 3 of the Stage 1 CLE programme. Both the spoken and the written discourse are supported by the context; and, moreover, they support each other. These conditions are favourable for learning to discourse in both modes of the language at the same time. The demand is low, for both modes, because both the spoken and the written language are heavily scaffolded. Moreover, the teacher can reinforce that scaffolding, by gesture, by using the spoken language to help understanding of the written text, and so on, enabling all the students to participate, whether or not they are familiar with the language of instruction.

Conclusion

When teachers with a traditional orientation first witness good CLE teaching the most frequent reaction is amazement at what the students read and write. To some, it is unbelievable that Grade 3 students in a Khmer-speaking, Buriram school, for example, write copiously in standard Thai, including writing beautiful poetry. Probably the most valuable lesson of all, to be learnt from this extensive field experience with CLE techniques in educationally difficult regions, is that the placing of limits on what children should learn and when they should learn it is destructive of learning.

In the past, texts were graded for difficulty in regard to such things as the length of words, the number of words per sentence, and the type, length and complexity of sentences and paragraphs. In addition, the difficulty level of texts that students encountered within reading programmes was carefully controlled. The great error was that teachers then came to believe that students of a particular age were not capable of more than that, and that ability to read and write had to be developed in the sequence that was set down by these arbitrarily imposed limitations.

CLE teaching places no such limits on the difficulty of what a child is allowed to read or write. While children are learning to speak their mother tongue, within the home, they learn to do amazingly difficult and complex things with language, in a very short time. No one places limits there on what they should try to learn. Once children are placed within circumstances where they become enthusiastic readers and writers, they will learn to do things that are similarly amazing, if we do not place limits on what they are allowed to do. In that case, the discrepancy between failure rates in learning to use the spoken and written modes of language that was referred to in Chapter 1 may well diminish – in the best possible way.

References

Brisbane College of Advanced Education (BCAE) (1982) *The Mount Gravatt Developmental Language Reading Program.* Syndey: Addison-Wesley.

Cazden, C.B. (1977) Concentrated versus contrived encounters: suggestions for language assessment in early childhood education. In A. Davies (ed.) *Language Learning in Early Childhood.* London: Heinemann.

Chapman, L.J. (1987) 'Report to Rotary International on the Thailand Pilot Literacy Project'. Manuscript.

Gray, B. (1980) *Developing Language and Literacy with Urban Aboriginal Children.* A first report on the Traeger Park Project presented at Conference 80/2. Darwin: Northern Territory, Department of Education.

Gray, B. (1983) *Helping Children become Language Learners in the Classroom.* A paper delivered at the annual conference of the Meanjin Reading Council, Brisbane, May.

Halliday, M.A.K. (1973) *Explorations in the Functions of Language.* London: Edward Arnold.

Halliday, M.A.K. and Hasan, R. (1985) *Language, Context and Text: A Social Semiotic Perspective.* Geelong: Deakin University Press.

Morris, A. and Stewart-Dore, N. (1984) *Learning to Learn from Text.* Sydney: Addison-Wesley.

Mount Gravatt Developmental Language Reading Program (1982) *Language at Work, Level 5 and Level 6.* Sydney: Addison-Wesley.

Rattanavich, S. and Walker, R.F. (1990) The Rotary Literacy in Thailand Project. *Education for All: Report of the UNESCO South East Asia and South Pacific Regional Conference.* Darwin: Northern Territory Department of Education.

Rotary International (1987) 3-H Literacy Project in Thailand. *Project Application to the Rotary Foundation of Rotary International.* Evanston: The Rotary Foundation of Rotary International.

Smith, F.C. (1982) *Writing and the Writer.* New York: Holt.

Smith, R.J. and Johnson, D.D. (1976) *Teaching Children to Read.* Reading: Addison-Wesley.

Walker, R.F. (1981) *The Language of Entering Children at Traeger Park School.* Occasional Paper No. 11. Canberra: The Australian Curriculum Development Centre.

Walker, R.F. and Rattanavich, S. (1987) *The Concentrated Language Encounter Programme at Srinakharinwirot University.* A paper presented at the Regional English Language Centre Seminar: The Role of Language Education in Human Resource Development. Singapore, 13–16 April.

Wells, G. (1981) *Learning through Interaction: The Study of Language Development.* Cambridge: Cambridge University Press.

Wickert, R. (1989) *No Single Measure: A Survey of Australian Adult Literacy.* Canberra: Commonwealth Department of Employment, Education and Training.

Index